MUNSTER OUR ROAD TO GLORY

MUNSTER
OUR ROAD
TO GLORY

Alan English with the Munster team

Photographs by Billy Stickland and Inpho

PENGUIN
IRELAND

PENGUIN IRELAND

Published by the Penguin Group
Penguin Ireland, 25 St Stephen's Green, Dublin 2, Ireland
(a division of Penguin Books Ltd)
Penguin Books Ltd, 80 Strand, London WC2R OLR, England
Penguin Group (USA) Inc., 375 Hudson Street, New York, New York 10014, USA
Penguin Group (Australia), 250 Camberwell Road,
Camberwell, Victoria 3124, Australia (a division of Pearson Australia Group Pty Ltd)
Penguin Group (Canada), 90 Eglinton Avenue East, Suite 700, Toronto, Ontario, Canada M4P 2Y3
(a division of Pearson Penguin Canada Inc.)
Penguin Books India Pvt Ltd, 11 Community Centre,
Panchsheel Park, New Delhi – 110 017, India
Penguin Group (NZ), 67 Apollo Drive, Mairangi Bay, Auckland 1310,
New Zealand (a division of Pearson New Zealand Ltd)
Penguin Books (South Africa) (Pty) Ltd, 24 Sturdee Avenue,
Rosebank, Johannesburg 2196, South Africa
Penguin Books Ltd, Registered Offices: 80 Strand, London WC2R OLR, England

www.penguin.com

First published 2006
1

Copyright © Alan English, 2006
Photographs copyright © Inpho/Solidus except 176, 217, 251 copyright © Inpho/Getty Images
(see page 286 for photo credits)

The moral right of the author has been asserted

Set in Garage Gothic, Minion and Trade Gothic
Designed and typeset by Smith & Gilmour, London
Printed in Great Britain by Butler & Tanner Ltd, Frome and London

A CIP catalogue record for this book is available from the British Library

ISBN-13 978-1-844-88133-8
ISBN-10 1-844-88133-4

CONTENTS

NO HOLDING BACK

'LET'S HAVE A RIGHT CUT OFF IT'

DONNCHA O'CALLAGHAN: When I was a boy in Cork, playing rugby for my school, I came across something on the pitch one day after I'd scored a try. I bent down and picked it up: it was a holy cross, on a chain. I stuffed it into my pocket. I still have it and I've never cleaned it up – there are probably still bits of the Christians pitch stuck to it. I keep the chain in an old make-up jar my sister gave me. In there I've got a few religious things that are important to me. The lads slag me over the jar. That's the Munster way. Every now and then my mum picks up some holy water and puts a bit in there. I consider myself religious. Not in a big way – I'm not a religious freak or anything – but often I take the cross out of its jar and say a prayer to give thanks for the great family I have, for everything that has happened to me through rugby, for putting me in a dressing room like ours. There's bound to be fellas out there that are as talented, if not more talented, than me. I know I've been lucky.

I'd never prayed to ask for anything, but before the Biarritz match I did. I was about to pray as I normally would, but then I remember thinking, 'Please, just let us win this game.' I almost wanted to say sorry for doing it, for asking about a rugby match. It was probably the wrong way to feel. But it meant so much to me, my family and my friends.

PETER STRINGER: It's funny the things that go through your head the night before a match, just lying awake in bed. I imagined us pressing for a try in the last minute of the final. We're awarded a penalty, but three points are no good to us – we need five. I have the ball when the referee blows his whistle, just a few yards from touch. It's obvious we have to go for the lineout. But do I have the right to tap the ball out? Ronan always does that. It's his job. But we're only a few feet away. Do I wait for him to come all the

way up and kick it out? I know it's kind of silly, but things like that creep into my mind.

Sometimes as well I try to get the feeling of what it would be like to dive over the line unchallenged and score a try, the feeling of touching the ball off the ground and my body landing a split-second later. In my head I want to feel what it's like because I'd never done that. I'd see people do it on the TV and I'd think, 'Jesus, I'd love to do that, I'd love to try it.' Over the years I'd had a few chances, but I always just touched the ball down. I never dived. So I had to keep replaying it in my mind in bed and I don't think I ever got it, that feeling of hitting the ground. I kept trying to imagine it, because I would think to myself, 'If I don't get that feeling now I'm not going to score the try.'

RONAN O'GARA: The night before the final it lashed rain, and I had a few negative thoughts. I'd played there before when the roof was closed. With the amount of people in the stadium, there can be a condensation effect. I had that memory in my head.

I was fearful of having dew on the ball. I don't like a wet ball – it's a lot easier to pass a dry one. Then I only got to kick at one end of the pitch the day before. We weren't given enough time, and I was kicked off the pitch. That might have upset me before, but I'm stronger now.

That night we had our team meeting, and Anthony Foley spoke. Munster means everything to him. I could probably count on one hand the fellas I'd be prepared to die for, and he'd be one of them. There's a few like that who are special, I suppose.

ANTHONY FOLEY: That afternoon I had to do a press conference with the Biarritz captain, Lièvremont. They wanted a snap of the two of us holding the cup, but I said no. I've always firmly believed that if you want a cup you have to earn the right to lift it. There's no point in touching it or rubbing it until you've earned it. We hadn't done that.

At the team meeting I tried to make some basic points. I told them we shouldn't be waiting for it to happen, we had to be the ones who went out there and played. I said,

> **I HAD TO CUT MYSELF SHORT BECAUSE I COULD HEAR THE EMOTION COMING THROUGH IN MY VOICE. I COULD FEEL IT RISING INSIDE ME. IT'S IMPORTANT THAT YOU DON'T GET TOO CARRIED AWAY THE NIGHT BEFORE — WE'D MADE THAT MISTAKE BEFORE.**

'Lads, I've woken up on the Sunday morning after two Heineken Cup finals with nothing but regrets. We can't let that happen this time, we can't be wishing we'd done things differently. Let's have a right cut off it. Let's leave nothing on the pitch and see where that takes us.'

I had to cut myself short because I could hear the emotion coming through in my voice. I could feel it rising inside me. It's important that you don't get too carried away the night before – we'd made that mistake before. I was thinking, 'Get your point across. Don't labour it. You don't want to get into that state again.'

PAUL O'CONNELL: You always know when Axel is getting emotional. You can see his lips quivering. Mick Galwey used to be like that as well – he used to have the tears and Claw used to have the tears and it's brilliant, like. Just seeing how much it means to people.

We knew there would be 70,000 Munster people there the following day and we knew what it meant to them, too. In Munster, you can never get away from that and you wouldn't want to. On the Wednesday before myself and Axel went to B&Q to get a piece of wood for the bottom of my wardrobe, so I could put one set of shoes under it and another set over it. Just getting the shoes off the ground, like. That's the type of thing you do – a stupid little job but sure it would kill an afternoon. Rather that than sitting down and looking at their lineouts for the fifteenth time.

Of course, we ended up having photos taken with the whole staff. First as a group, then individually. People are coming up and patting you on the back, wishing you well. You're thinking, 'God, things are gone mad,' but at the same time you've got to

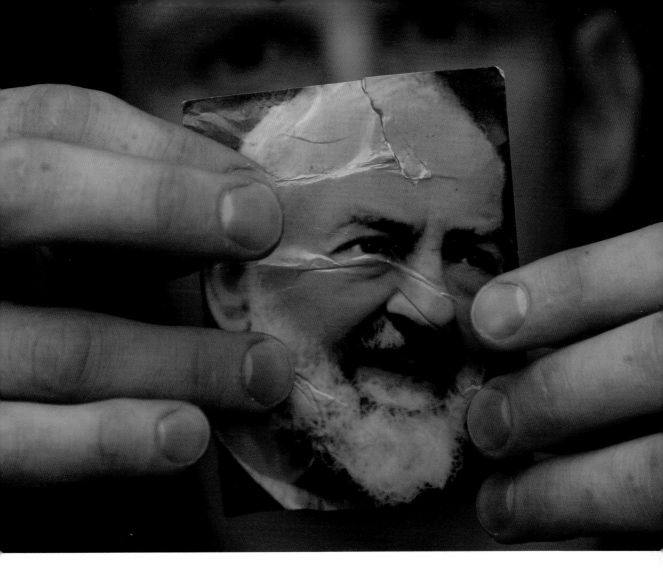

keep your feet on the ground and your head in the right place. You know the atmosphere is crazy, you know it's like nothing you've ever seen before, but through the experience you've built up you realize you're getting there in good shape mentally.

Physically, I'd had a terrible build-up. I went over on my ankle playing a Celtic League match in Wales fifteen days before the final and tore a ligament. The ankle swelled up and went black and blue. Up to five days before the match I was thinking, 'I'm in trouble here,' but then it started to feel stronger, and I was just hoping it would hold out. My mother gave me a picture of Padre Pio to wear under my sock in the final. You know the way you give money to Padre Pio? He did well out of me that week. My parents and friends and relations had him well funded.

DONNCHA O'CALLAGHAN: Paulie sets the standards in our squad. I don't think I can describe how much I respect him. People will say that I mess around a bit, but when I get out on the pitch I'd like to think I want it just as much as him. I take my rugby very seriously. I have to do everything the right way. The lads slag me off for being superstitious, but I'm not. It's just that before a match there are little things I like to have done and have out of the way. I say my prayer. I always have the same training kit with me. I wear the same pair of jocks. I always have a new pair of short white socks that I wear under my rugby socks – it's something I've done since playing for the school.

PAUL O'CONNELL: I read a lot of sports books, one after the other. A lot of them are rubbish, but sometimes you pick up something helpful. In his book, Steve Redgrave says superstitions hold you back. I totally believe that. I mean, are you going to train your ass off for six months and then play like a bag of shite because you forgot your lucky shorts or you didn't get to go out second?

DONNCHA O'CALLAGHAN: Paulie says to me, 'What would happen if you didn't have the new pair of socks?' I'm always telling him that would never happen. I'd never be that under-prepared – I always have them packed and ready to go. I don't accept that I'm superstitious. OK, maybe I'm fighting it hard – but I'd never give in to O'Connell.

MICK GALWEY: That Friday night in Cardiff, you had to be there to believe the level of anticipation. People were arriving from all over the world, on boats, planes, cars and buses, even motorbikes. There were people who just had to be there, no matter what. And because I had captained Munster in two finals, they all seemed to think that I was the expert.

'Well, Mick, are we going to do it?'

'Well, Gaillimh, is this our year at last?'

And what could I say but, 'We will. We will, yeah. We'll do it this time.'

All I could think was, 'God, if the players could only see what an effort people have made here. If they could only see the excitement, it would do them the world of good. I wish they could see and realize at first-hand what it means to everybody.' Because when you're in the camp, you're aware of it, but you don't fully realize it. You have to be on the outside again to fully grasp it. Some of these fans who put on Munster jerseys are half-thinking they're going to be called in as a sub on the Saturday, they're that close to the team. Ready to play if they have to.

There was a monkey on our backs. I was never more aware of it than that night in Cardiff. I never wanted to be associated with a team that lost two Heineken Cup finals and never came back to win it.

ROB HENDERSON: There was electricity in the team room. If we could have played it then, we would have done. We were totally ready. But we understood the emotion that was there and we knew how to handle it better this time. Some of us were on the bench, plenty of other guys were going to be in the stand, but we were all in it together.

Playing for Munster is different. It reminds me of my early days in the game, before we started getting paid. The reason you were playing rugby was for each other and for the club and for the people who came and supported us. And that is exactly the same ethos that Munster have now. We turn up, we train together, we take the

> **PLAYING FOR MUNSTER IS DIFFERENT. IT REMINDS ME OF MY EARLY DAYS IN THE GAME, BEFORE WE STARTED GETTING PAID. THE REASON YOU WERE PLAYING RUGBY WAS FOR EACH OTHER AND FOR THE CLUB AND FOR THE PEOPLE WHO CAME AND SUPPORTED US. AND THAT IS EXACTLY THE SAME ETHOS THAT MUNSTER HAVE NOW.**

piss out of each other, we go for pints together, we go to the pictures together. In rugby, you don't have to be friends on and off the field – that's just the way it works out with Munster. If you're in, you're in. It's like a family club where everyone gets a share, not just the players, but the man on the street, the fans who keep propping the team up when it seems like it's a lost cause, the people who write the letters and the faxes – the thousands that we have received over ten years. All of those people have a small part of what Munster is.

After the team meeting you're just killing time, waiting for the moment when you get on the bus the next day. People get themselves ready in their own ways. Some guys mess around until late, other guys just stay away, and you won't see them until the team room the day of the match. Some sleep fine, with others the nerves start kicking in the night before.

Vale of Glamorgan Hotel, Friday, 19 May 2006
Room 110: Donncha O'Callaghan and Marcus Horan

MARCUS HORAN: Myself and Donners, we always chat the night before a match. I think one of us always wants the other to say, 'We'll be fine tomorrow.' One of us always says it.

I hadn't played a match for seven weeks, not since I'd injured my calf in training. I was worried, of course I was, but that night I said, 'Donners, I don't care if I don't finish the game. I'm going to go as hard as I can for as long as I can.'

I think he got a bit of a buzz off that. I got a bit of a buzz off what he was talking about, too. The fact that he couldn't eat either. I think it's good when you know that everyone is going through the same thing. It's important to have that. If he'd told me, 'I had a full dinner there, it was grand,' I wouldn't have felt very good.

Donners likes to get to bed early. It doesn't matter if he's chatting for two hours while he's in bed. He just likes to be under the sheets, settling down. I checked into our room first and straight away I knew there was going to be trouble. Somebody had put a ping-pong table directly outside our bedroom door. It was to help guys to relax the night before the final, and the only place it would fit was outside our door.

I knew Donners would freak. I heard him from inside the room when he realized, as he was walking down the corridor.

'Ah for fuck's sake!'

DONNCHA O'CALLAGHAN: Some plonker put a table-tennis table outside our room. It was a disaster. I was about to have a nap when it started.

Bop, bop, bop, bop, bop, bop …

First of all I thought, 'I'll take it handy here. They won't hang around, we're playing the European Cup final tomorrow.' So I buried my head in the pillow. Half an hour later, I could hear the crowd arriving, the roars, the cheers. I stuck my head outside the door.

'Lads, keep it down will ye? We're trying to get some sleep here.'

They ignored me. I stuck my head under the pillow again. I was thinking, 'This can't be happening.' So then I sent Marcus out to quieten them. The enforcer.

MARCUS HORAN: I went out there and of course eejit here got roped into it. Denis Fogarty was playing Tomas O'Leary, and I ended up taking on the winner.

DONNCHA O'CALLAGHAN: I still had my head under the pillow, but it was getting worse. Then there was the biggest roar of all. I jumped out of bed, opened the door, and there he was, holding a bat. Marcus.

'What the hell are *you* doing out there?'

MARCUS HORAN: I was like a kid being caught red-handed with a packet of sweets. I just said, 'Look, if you can't beat them, join them.' He came out then and made me help him move the ping-pong table down to the other end of the corridor and fold it up, but after a while the lads moved it back and started playing again. He'd had enough at that stage.

DONNCHA O'CALLAGHAN: It came to the stage where I was thinking, 'To hell with this. It's more important that I get a rest than they play table tennis. So I hid the ball in my room. Even after they stopped, I could still hear it in my head for a while.

Bop, bop, bop, bop, bop, bop ...

Room 101: Anthony Foley

I like to have my own room with Munster, otherwise I get a bit agitated. The private space helps me to clear my mind and think about what I'm going to say to the boys the next day. You've got to make sure that what you say doesn't have a negative effect on anyone. Some of us had been down this road a few times, but for a lot of them it was a new experience. You could easily say the wrong thing, if you weren't careful. It's important to get a good night's sleep as well. I got up just before midnight. I could hear pool balls clattering around the place. I opened the door and they started hiding – Mossy Lawlor and Ian Dowling. There was no point in roaring and shouting – you'd just wake up the other lads. But, ah, they finished up straight away after that.

Room 210: Declan Kidney

I heard about the ping-pong table, but there are some things you just back off from. When I was coaching school teams, I had a rule that, if I saw anybody smoking, I wasn't wasting my time training them. Three days before a Schools Cup final, I saw this fella coming down the road, with a cigarette. I ended up having to duck down in my car so I could just about see out the windscreen. Because if he knew that I'd seen him, I'd have to drop him.

Every fella in the Munster squad has his own way of getting himself up for a game. As coach, you try to hit it at the mean, the average. Where is that? There's no scientific way of knowing. It's a feel thing. You go with what you think is right. You're dealing with a lot of different people who bring a lot of different things to an occasion. You can't control all of that. Nobody can. You try to get all of those people working in the same direction, with the same focus. You're like a chef hoping the cake settles properly, that it's the right mix. There was never going to be an issue with getting fellas up for

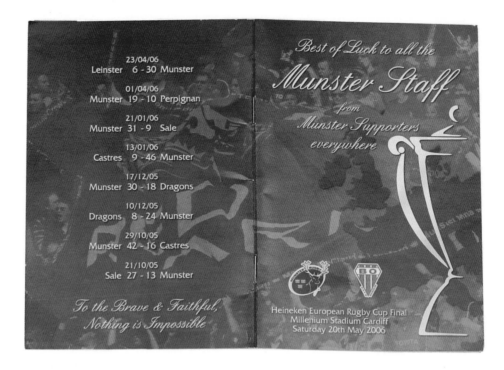

23/04/06
Leinster 6 - 30 Munster

01/04/06
Munster 19 - 10 Perpignan

21/01/06
Munster 31 - 9 Sale

13/01/06
Castres 9 - 46 Munster

17/12/05
Munster 30 - 18 Dragons

10/12/05
Dragons 8 - 24 Munster

29/10/05
Munster 42 - 16 Castres

21/10/05
Sale 27 - 13 Munster

*To the Brave & Faithful,
Nothing is Impossible*

Best of Luck to all the
Munster Staff
from
Munster Supporters
everywhere

Heineken European Rugby Cup Final
Millenium Stadium Cardiff
Saturday 20th May 2006

that game, it was just a case of keeping the lid on it in the weeks leading up to it. And now the time was coming to let the lid off.

That night in my room the text messages were coming in all the time. I was trying to do the right thing and reply to some of them. I went for a little walk, five or ten minutes around the car park. If there's somebody at a loose end, you stop and talk to them about whatever. I was just trying to keep an eye on things. Went back to the room then and I picked up the little book we were all given by the supporters' club. It was full of goodwill messages. Powerful messages.

'There are not many mornings that you wake up knowing that this is a day you have dreamed of for most of your life. The morning of the Heineken Cup final will be one of those mornings for you. Your performances have been an inspiration to everyone who dreams of becoming a champion. Now your own turn has come to be champions. Do not let the occasion overshadow the day. Take control of your fate and turn your dreams into reality.' – *Sean Óg Ó hAilpín*

'You make other sports people want to be better.' – *Sam Lynch*

'In all the years I've watched ye playing, I've never been so proud. Ye all deserve the cup this year and I say that with my hand on my heart. Best of luck and sow it into those French bastards.' – *Peter Clohessy*

'Lads, please take us out of our misery and bring the cup home.' – *Kenny Smith*

'WE MUST WIN! WE MUST WIN! WE MUST WIN!' – *Mark T. O'Brien*

Enough. Put the book down. Don't go there.

Room 103: Peter Stringer and David Wallace

PETER STRINGER: I'd been thinking about it all week, thinking about lifting the cup and how it would feel. There was very little negative thinking coming in. I never thought, 'Jesus, what if we lose this?' It was almost like we weren't going to play a final at all, that we were all going somewhere together, off on another holiday. It didn't have the pressure of a final. Not to me, anyway.

I'm not one to be going to bed too early – I try and get the last of the crack out of the day if there's anyone around. There's something about getting away from home. Even when guys are filtering off to bed I'm still giddy, looking for a bit of fun, until there's nobody left to play with. Then I go back to the room and try to annoy Wally.

When it's that close to the final, I'm jumping around the bed going, 'Come on! Can't wait for it! Bring it on!' And he was just lying there in bed, with his face pale white, saying, 'What are you doing? Why are you looking forward to this? It's so horrible.'

DAVID WALLACE: When the match is coming near, we are two different animals. Strings feeds off the fact that I'm a nervous wreck. I was petrified that night, and he enjoys watching me suffer. But I think he might relax me as well, in his own special way. The more nervous I am, the better it is for me on the day. I don't enjoy it – nobody could enjoy feeling like that – but I use it as a driving force.

❝WHEN IT'S THAT CLOSE TO THE FINAL, I'M JUMPING AROUND THE BED GOING, 'COME ON! CAN'T WAIT FOR IT! BRING IT ON!'❞

"I FEEL THAT TO GET THE BEST OUT OF WALLY, I'VE GOT TO DOMINATE HIM. SOMETIMES HE DOESN'T LIKE THAT."

The following morning I woke early – because of the day that was in it, I suppose. Like a kid at Christmas. I wanted to go and get an early breakfast, because I knew what Strings would be like. That's my routine, and you don't want to do anything different. You're into a schedule before you know it, four or five hours before the game.

RONAN O'GARA: Wally lost the plot on me at the lineout session after breakfast. I wanted him to move immediately he saw the ball leaving their Number 10's hands. I feel that to get the best out of Wally, I've got to dominate him. Sometimes he doesn't like that and he snapped at me. I could see his point of view. I knew he was trying to get himself right for three o'clock. I'm trying to get myself right too, and that's what happens.

I put my hand up. Me and Wally, we work so closely together on the pitch, and I depend on him a lot. If you asked me to pick a seven, he's the first fellow I'd have on my team, you know.

DAVID WALLACE: I like to get strapped early, then I go back to the room and listen to music for half an hour. I find it settles me, helps get me into the right mood. On the morning of a game everything is happening all around you. You've got to focus on yourself and your own thoughts, because you can get distracted by what's going on. You just want half an hour of clarity.

I flick around until I get a good song. I usually know straight away whether it's right. Sometimes I listen to 'Nothing Else Matters' by Metallica, but often a song will lose its impact the more I hear it, so I keep flicking away, trying to find the right one.

PETER STRINGER: Wally is the one guy in the squad who doesn't have an iPod. He's got one of these Creative things – he gets slagged because it looks like a cassette player. Very old school. For whatever reason, he won't upgrade it. He's sticking to his guns. The thing he has is on its last legs, and for it to work he has to bang it off the table.

He gets really annoyed with it sometimes, and that puts him in even more of a state. If that's possible.

DAVID WALLACE: Sometimes a song comes on that surprises you, a song you wouldn't think of until you hear the words. I remember 'In The Air Tonight' by Phil Collins coming on that morning. That got me going. I listened to it a couple of times …
I've been waiting for this moment all my life …

MARCUS HORAN: The bus journey to the game was very special. We had a motorcycle escort – four outriders. Normally the cops over there stop at the lights. In Ireland they stop for no one. This time, though, there was no stopping until we hit the city centre. Then we saw a sea of red in front of us. Even with my earphones in, I could hear the

bus rattling and the crowd shouting. There were guys with their fists in the air and tears in their eyes. Grown men crying right in front of us, more than an hour before the game. It suddenly hit me what I was about to experience, because the injury had been the only thing in my head all week. And I was just so thankful that I was able to experience it, and not have to watch from the stand. I was so happy that I was going to be togging out. Missing that day, when I'd been involved all season, would have broken my heart.

DECLAN KIDNEY: On the bus to the ground, the challenge was staying in the zone. I told them, 'Just enjoy the journey, lads. But remember. They can't make a tackle for you. They can't score a point for you.' But all the same, it was a hugely powerful experience. Seeing something like that makes these guys get up off the ground straight away when they've been hit. It makes them lean into the tackle that little bit stronger.

> **EVEN WITH MY EARPHONES IN, I COULD HEAR THE BUS RATTLING AND THE CROWD SHOUTING. THERE WERE GUYS WITH THEIR FISTS IN THE AIR AND TEARS IN THEIR EYES. GROWN MEN CRYING RIGHT IN FRONT OF US, MORE THAN AN HOUR BEFORE THE GAME.**

DAVID WALLACE: We drove through the gates, and I thought, 'OK – just forget about it now.' There were no more people on the side of the road shouting. It was just us now. Without anyone saying it, I think everyone else felt the same.

DONNCHA O'CALLAGHAN: Everyone was ready. At the team meeting earlier, Axel and John Kelly said some powerful things. Then Paulie spoke. I don't think there's much point in anyone talking after him. He always gets me right for a game. He talked about honesty. He talked about guys in the room being 100 per centers. He said the guys who weren't lucky enough to tog out were 100 per centers too. He said that was the difference between us and other teams. I knew that he was right, and I knew that everything he said he was going to back up on the pitch. That was huge for me.

PAUL O'CONNELL: I didn't have to worry about anyone not giving it everything. If Biarritz wanted it, they were going to have to show up and beat us. Because we weren't going to hold anything back. We went out for the final in 2002 and I think we played not to lose. We were playing to win this time. We had to go for it from the very first second.

There are a lot of clichés out there but plenty of them become clichés because they're actually very true. Things like 'you can't buy experience'. You just can't. We had lost two finals. The guys who were beaten in 2000 know now that they were a bit overawed by the whole thing, but if you'd asked them back then, they would probably have said, 'No, we weren't overawed.'

Experience isn't something you measure. You can't say, 'Right, because I played in that final I have the experience to handle this one. I know now that I have to do this,

this and this, but not that.' It's not like that: you just find yourself handling it. But we were only in that position because of everything that had gone before.

PETER STRINGER: I get my excitement from the atmosphere at big games. As a kid I loved watching the build-up to the FA Cup final. I loved all the flags, the people singing, the banners in the crowd. Even now, at the end of a match like that, I want the commentators to shut up. I don't want to hear them, I want to listen to the crowd singing. If it was up to me I'd turn all the cameras on the fans and keep them rolling, to see if you could pick up that atmosphere. It makes the hairs stand up on the back of my neck. I'd always kind of dream of having that myself.

Walking out on to the pitch at Cardiff for the warm-up was unbelievable. Long before the kick-off the stadium was nearly full with our fans. I'd like to have walked around ten times, just to feel that energy and hear everyone in the ground singing the same song. You just get a sense that everyone is there for the same purpose, and you can feel the energy they're giving out.

We got back to the dressing room and there were guys pottering around – squad members and coaches and physios. Then Axel said, 'Look, this is our time – the fifteen guys going out on the pitch.'

We were left on our own then, in a huddle, a tight huddle. Shoulders back and chests out. There were no heads down – guys were looking at each other in the eye. It's not always like that, in rugby. Sometimes guys are sick with anticipation and worry, doubting themselves. Sometimes a guy will break the huddle and you can hear him getting sick in the background. This time, everyone was totally focused. It was the most emotional get-together we'd had all week. You looked across at the guy facing you and you knew he had given everything in preparation. A few people spoke. John Kelly said he would never want to be in another dressing room, that he couldn't have picked a better bunch of lads to go and play rugby with. Axel spoke, and I'd never seen him like that before. What came across was his own realization that this could be his last chance to win it. You could really feel that and you could see how much it meant to him.

I was thinking, 'I don't want to wake up in the morning and look at myself and say I could have given more.' There was so much on the line for us, we'd been through so much over the years. It's one thing letting yourself down, but if you let down someone else you know you'll never forgive yourself. There was a real sense of that feeling in the huddle. We were going to go out and give everything we had inside us. We were going out there to win.

CHAPTER 1
BEGINNINGS

❝ CAN WE AT LEAST KEEP IT UNDER FIFTY POINTS? ❞

1 November 1995

Nobody could have suspected it was the beginning of an epic journey: not the players, not the newspapers, not any of the six or seven thousand who turned up on a Wednesday afternoon at Thomond Park for Munster's first match in the inaugural Heineken European Cup.

They were different days. Professionalism was on its way: the first contracts to be offered to Irish rugby players were being prepared. For many in Ireland, the transition would be painful. 'Amateurism as we knew it is dead, and I greatly regret it,' said Billy Lavery of the Irish Rugby Football Union. In England, the pace of change was faster. Agents appeared from nowhere, alive to the quick buck, hovering over the carrion of amateur Irish rugby.

In Munster there was talk of superclubs – how else to compete with the giants from England already eyeing up the best players in a province that had dominated the All Ireland League from day one? Club rugby was everything. The provincial side had a storied history – decades of epic battles and famous victories against the overseas teams – but a questionable future. In the brave new world, the likes of the All Blacks and the Springboks didn't have the time or the inclination to stop off at places like Thomond Park any more. With only the other Irish provinces to play against, Munster had emerged from a long slump, but not many had noticed, or cared. Professionalism would change that.

Between the provinces and the clubs there could only be one winner in the new era. There was never going to be enough money in the pot to put both on a professional footing. There were too many clubs for professionalism to be viable, something the game in Wales and Scotland would find to its cost in later years.

Peter Clohessy and Mick Galwey in Munster's first-ever European Cup match, a 17–13 victory over Swansea at Thomond Park, 1 November 1995

They would end up creating regional sides, which would face widespread resistance. Ireland already had four recognized regions – the provinces – so the transition was never going to be such a hard sell. It took a while, but slowly the influence of Ireland's clubs waned and the provinces began to prosper, Munster and Ulster in particular.

The clubs of England did not enter the new European competition in its inaugural year – they could not find room for it in their season – but twelve teams from five countries kicked it off without them. From France there were Toulouse, Begles-Bordeaux and Castres. From Wales came Cardiff, Swansea and Pontypridd. Romania were in, represented by Farul Constanta. So were Italy, who sent out Milan and Benetton Treviso. And from Ireland, there was Ulster, Leinster and Munster. Rank outsiders all.

MICK GALWEY: There had been talk about this European Cup. People were curious. What would it be like? That afternoon they weren't exactly coming in over the walls

> # YOU COULD TELL SWANSEA WERE WELL AHEAD OF US IN TERMS OF CONDITIONING. THEY WERE GETTING READY FOR PROFESSIONALISM. WE WEREN'T SURE WHAT WAS HAPPENING AT THAT STAGE. 🔲

at Thomond Park, but we were surprised at the amount of people who showed up. This was Munster. We were used to playing in front of small crowds in the interpros. Club rugby was our bread and butter. But all of a sudden we had a younger side coming through, a back row of Eddie Halvey, Anthony Foley and David Corkery, and we thought we might able to do a bit of damage.

JERRY HOLLAND: I was the Munster coach that day. I watched the match from the far embankment – there was acres of room over there. You could tell Swansea were well ahead of us in terms of conditioning. They were getting ready for professionalism. We weren't sure what was happening at that stage. We were trying to create a little bit of ownership of the players, tapping into what the clubs had achieved, not taking from them. The Heineken Cup was the new frontier.

We struggled all the way through that match, hanging on in there. Right at the end, when it looked like we were beaten, Pat Murray scored a great try under the posts to win it for us. That was it, the start of our unbeaten record in Thomond Park.

A week later we went over to play Castres. The match was in a place called Mazamet, and the ground was like a bowl with high wiring all around. There were bands playing in four different corners. I'd never seen such hostility. It wasn't hatred. It was just bordering on that.

ANTHONY FOLEY: Fellas were getting gouged and kicked and the whole lot. We were going, 'Jesus, calm down will ye? It's only a game, like.' I remember Kenny Smith going up to take a penalty. He was a phenomenal kicker but he barely made contact with the ball. The noise was unreal – he was used to getting absolute silence in Thomond Park. But

FELLAS WERE GETTING GOUGED AND KICKED AND THE WHOLE LOT. WE WERE GOING, 'JESUS, CALM DOWN WILL YE?'

we played well. We weathered the storm. In the last minute it was 12–12 and they were pressing us, but we had a chance of a breakout. I'll never forget Corks – David Corkery – sold a dummy to me and got tackled and turned over the ball. They scored a try in the other corner, and it turned out afterwards that if we'd held on for the draw we'd have qualified for the semi-final. That was it, then. Our season was over.

Early in 1996, a select group of Ireland internationals were given full-time professional contracts. The union had no choice: offers from England were now pouring in. Harlequins came for the brilliant Garryowen hooker Keith Wood – and landed him. Some, among them Munster's Jerry Holland, argued that offering deals to international regulars was never going to stem the flow of talent – there had to be a system put in place at provincial level. A squad of players on union contracts. Professionalism in the provinces.

'I have no comment to make on their opinions,' the IRFU president Bobby Deacy told Brendan Fanning in *The Sunday Times*. 'I don't know what they mean by provincial contracts, and I don't know if they know what they mean by provincial contracts.'

In October, the European Cup came around again, and this time the English clubs deigned to enter. Munster, drawn in a pool with Toulouse, Wasps, Cardiff and Milan, were viewed as having no chance of qualifying, a judgement seemingly confirmed when they were beaten 48–18 in Cardiff. Wasps came to Thomond Park three days later, expecting to win. They were hammered. Something special happened that Saturday, a fury was unleashed, and Munster would call on it many times in the years ahead. Wasps, led by Lawrence Dallaglio, never stood a chance.

TOM ENGLISH, *THE SUNDAY TIMES*: Amid lusty howls of 'kill them!' bedlam broke out. From deep in their own half, Munster cut loose. Mick Galwey, their inspirational captain, took a fine lineout catch and drove 20 yards downfield. From the ensuing ruck, Killian Keane hoisted a garryowen into the drizzly skies, and a wobbly Paul Sampson lost it in the air. The Munster pack arrived in numbers, and the imperious Foley emerged with the ball under his arm. The Shannon man drove with all his might for the Wasps line and eventually got there, half of the visiting team hanging out of him as he crashed over for a try. Cue raucous celebrations and cue, also, wholesale panic in the Wasps ranks.

MICK GALWEY: Two weeks later we went to Toulouse. The previous week, Wasps had beaten them by sixty points. We had given Wasps a hiding, so God help us we reckoned we had a great chance.

They came at us in droves. They started running in tries at will. Fellas were doing their best, but their best wasn't good enough. We weren't fit enough, cute enough, hard enough or experienced enough. Christian Califano scored at least two tries. He'd appear like this big bloody monster after a rolling maul and we couldn't put a hand on him. After about the sixth try, I got the lads together under the posts. At that stage the game was long gone – so what do you say as a captain? I mean, we're not going to win this one, you know? But sure, I made a speech anyway …

'For fuck's sake, lads, can we at least keep it under fifty points? Because we have to go home and face the crowd after this.'

They scored three more tries. The final score was 60–19, I'll never forget it. The most important thing we did out of that game was to learn from it. It was the best wake-up call Munster ever got.

In March 1997 it was announced that John Bevan, the former Wales and Lions wing, was to be Munster's first professional coach. One month later, the player drain reached its height. In the same week that David Corkery left Munster for Bristol, in a deal reputedly worth up £200,000 over three years, the IRFU finally revealed its plans for provincial contracts.

WE WEREN'T FIT ENOUGH, CUTE ENOUGH, HARD ENOUGH OR EXPERIENCED ENOUGH.

'Interprovincial players,' reported Edmund van Esbeck in *The Irish Times*, 'will have the capacity to earn over £12,000. The four provinces can each contract thirty players and they will be paid a basic retainer of £5,000. Each player will get a match fee of £350 for warm-up matches, £450 for interprovincial championship matches and £800 for each appearance in the European Cup … Work is still being done on the contracts for those in other areas, including those for the senior international squad.'

When the Munster players heard this news, they were not impressed. It then emerged that Anthony Foley and Eddie Halvey, who had been on Ireland contracts with a £30,000 retainer the previous year, were to have their have basic salary cut to £15,000. Mick Galwey, who had been on a similar deal, had his international contract taken away completely.

JERRY HOLLAND: They were very uncertain times, difficult times for everybody. Players were concerned about their careers, their income, their livelihood. It's fair to say that everybody was nervous in terms of what direction it was going to go in – whether it was financially sustainable. Not just in paying the players, but in terms of the whole support system around them.

The provinces knew the direction we wanted to go in. We wanted to give players the opportunity to be full-time. That opportunity existed in England. There was a training session in Thomond Park, and I introduced John Bevan, who was taking over as Munster coach. He put forward his vision, told the players where he was going. But I think he was surprised by their reaction. He hadn't had a whole lot of contact with the IRFU; he didn't know then what their plans were. The union felt that at provincial level you could have a full-time director of rugby and a lot of part-time players. But that was never going to work. The players wanted to give themselves every chance.

That night, a number of the players decided they weren't going to get the kind of contract here that they needed. They wouldn't have been able to sustain themselves.

Anthony Foley

A lot of them said, 'Look we're going across the water. We have offers in the UK, and that's where we feel we need to go to make a career of this.' Not surprisingly, John Bevan found that a little bit disconcerting. So in the end he decided he was going to stay in Wales. They went for Andy Leslie after that – but he decided he was going to stay in New Zealand.

MICK GALWEY: All of a sudden I went from having thirty grand and a car to having nothing. There were a lot of offers floating around at that time. People were getting agents and God knows what. London Irish contacted me seven years on the trot, but I never really wanted to go away. Around that time, I was forced to think about it but I suppose I was a home bird, simple as that. My gut feeling told me not to do it. If it meant giving up professional rugby and sticking with Shannon, I would rather have done that. As things panned out, some of us were offered £25,000. They took the wheels away from us and we were docked five grand but we still had a job. I bit their hand off.

ANTHONY FOLEY: I talked to Harlequins and I talked to Sale and I was talking to Coventry. It was a fairly OK package – it wouldn't have made me a millionaire, but it was OK. One of the conditions was that I was allowed to play for Munster, but then something happened where I wouldn't have been able to. So I decided I wasn't going.

JERRY HOLLAND: Ultimately it was probably a gun to the head, but provincial contracts were set up, players became professional and a support structure was put in place to help them.

ALAN QUINLAN: I started playing rugby when I was eight or nine at Clanwilliam, the fourth-oldest club in the country, in Tipperary town. My dad and my uncles played there. Nicky English was my idol growing up. He lived up the road and he taught me in secondary school. Even when he was hurling for Tipperary he used to do his dad's coal round. He'd collect me after school and we'd deliver coal together. I never thought I'd take the rugby path, but, looking back, rugby was always first for me, deep down. I joined Shannon Under-20s, and things starting taking off for me.

I left my job in December 1996 because I knew Munster contracts were going to be given out the following year – some full-time, some part-time. I'd been a mechanic for five years in Pierse Motors, Tipperary town. At my going-away party people were

Declan Kidney in 1997

> # A JOURNALIST ASKED ME IF WE HAD ANY CHANCE. I THOUGHT THE GUY WAS ASKING ME IF WE HAD ANY CHANCE OF WINNING [THE CUP]. HE WASN'T. HE WAS TALKING ABOUT WINNING A MATCH.

asking me where I was off to. I said I was going training. On my own. They laughed at me, they thought I was crazy. But I knew I had a talent and I wanted to get ahead of the posse. I went to the gym every day up until June 1997, to get myself ready. I took a chance, really. I sold lotto tickets and did bits of part-time work. One day my mum rang me to say two letters had arrived for me, from the IRFU and the Munster branch. I told her to open them. There was a contract there for £7,500, plus match fees. The letter said, 'Please indicate if you will accept.' It was like a dream come true. To be paid for playing rugby. Unbelievable.

DECLAN KIDNEY: I was coaching Dolphin that year and looking after the teams at the school where I taught, Pres in Cork. I was asked if I'd come in and help Niall O'Donovan and Jerry Holland with the Munster team. I was just sort of put there, like. John Bevan had cried off, so it was just a case of, 'Will you come in and give a hand?'

After we'd played Ulster in the interpros, the Heineken Cup was coming up, and a journalist asked me if we had any chance. I thought the guy was asking me if we had any chance of winning it. He wasn't. He was talking about winning a match. That annoyed me then, but if you think back, it was perfectly understandable.

For the 1997–98 season, Munster were in a pool with Keith Wood's Harlequins, Cardiff and Bourgoin. For the first time, teams had to play each other home and away, as the tournament grew in size and stature. 'There are nine sides that can win this,' said the Leicester coach Bob Dwyer at the outset. 'The French quartet, the English teams and Cardiff.' You could get odds of 100–1 against Munster, Leinster or Ulster lifting the cup.

Munster travelled to London on Friday 6 September to take on Harlequins in their first pool match.

Opposite: **Alan Quinlan**

ALAN QUINLAN: I was nervous but excited to be playing for Munster. In the couple of months before that, I'd had a rough time of it. I had my part-time contract, but I wasn't getting picked. I'd wanted it so much and I didn't know what to do. Mick Galwey told me to keep the head down, to work harder. I knew I was good enough. I just needed the chance to prove it and I got it that day.

Woody was playing for Harlequins; they had Laurent Cabannes in their back row, and I felt a bit nervous being among these players. Johnny Lacey, one of my best friends, was on the wing, and our families were over there. It was a big thing for them and for us. We ended up losing 48–40, but it was a great experience. We didn't qualify from our pool, but we were learning all the time. Suddenly I had a bit of interest from English clubs, but I never got too excited about getting money over there. I decided to stay and learn my trade with Munster, and it was the best decision I ever made. They put me on full-time contract, and that was it, then. I was a professional rugby player.

DECLAN KIDNEY: Two weeks after we were knocked out, they wanted to know if I'd go for the job as full-time coach. I was asked to do a presentation the morning after Ireland played the All Blacks at Lansdowne Road. All I wanted to do was not let myself down. I loved my teaching job, I was working with some smashing people and I'd been there all my life, so there was no huge reason to change. But all of a sudden you have a chance to coach one team for a living, when I was involved with eighteen teams for nothing.

I had a lot of theories at the time about what should happen at underage level and right up through the system. To make my points, I had a flip chart, a presentation on an overhead projector, a video of different teams I'd trained. I asked them for aids to help me do the presentation but when I got there the hotel didn't have them. They managed to get me a board for the flip chart and a projector, but no TV for the video. There were eight or nine people there, and after I'd gone through the presentation I put the video up on the table and I told them, 'I put this together to show you but unfortunately I can't now.' Finished the interview and walked out of there in a sweat, thinking, 'Phew, I think that might have gone OK.'

The night before, I'd stayed at my brother Aidan's house in Dublin and before I went to bed I had checked that everything was in order. Checked the acetate sheet for the overhead – fine. Looked over the flip chart – fine. Put the video in, just to make sure the tape was at precisely the right point, and up on the screen came Barney, the purple dinosaur. My young fella had swapped the tapes. So it was very nearly a case of me putting on the video in the interview, sitting back and seeing Barney singing: 'I love you, you love me …'

A few weeks later I got a phone call to say the job was mine. I asked to think about it. For a month then I had kids coming in asking me for career guidance, and it was going through my head, 'What the hell am *I* going to do?' I decided to go for it, and we agreed a start date: 1 February 1998.

When it was announced, somebody asked me how long I'd be doing it for. I said: 'Three years or three losses – whichever comes first.' I just wanted everyone to give it their best. If you do that, then by definition you are a winner no matter what happens. Because a lot of people don't.

KILLIAN KEANE: It was probably a nightmare situation for Deccie to come into. He was regarded with a little bit of suspicion by some people. He didn't know us, and we didn't know him. Just because you're paid to do something doesn't mean you're a professional. You could argue that the professional attitude took four years to bed in.

We were setting for good performances on the road. Thomond Park was our fortress, but we didn't really believe we could win away. We had these teams on a pedestal, the likes of Toulouse. There was nobody there who could say, 'Look, we're actually better than this. We can beat these teams.'

JOHN KELLY: The following season we were better. It was first time we won away, against Padova in Italy. I think we had five supporters there that day, including my parents and Anthony Horgan's. They became known as the Padova Five. That season was the first

WHEN IT WAS ANNOUNCED, SOMEBODY ASKED ME HOW LONG I'D BE DOING IT FOR. I SAID: 'THREE YEARS OR THREE LOSSES — WHICHEVER COMES FIRST.'

THOMOND PARK WAS OUR FORTRESS, BUT WE DIDN'T REALLY BELIEVE WE COULD WIN AWAY.

time we got out of our group. We got an away draw in the quarter-final, against Colomiers. Did we really think, deep down, that we could go over there and beat them? No, we didn't.

But then something happened, and it changed everything. Keith Wood came back from Harlequins. John Langford came from Australia. Mike Mullins came from New Zealand. And Jason Holland – he came out of nowhere. He was a New Zealander playing for Midleton in Division Two of the All Ireland League. All of a sudden, it started to take off for us.

ANTHONY FOLEY: The new guys couldn't understand why we weren't going out to try and win the tournament. Why weren't we? I suppose because it was still unknown territory for us. You'd always have that bit of doubt. 'Oh, we're Irish, maybe we're not good enough.' But then we started to get a decent squad together. Ronan and Peter were coming through. We were really looking forward to the next campaign. We thought we might be able to do something this time.

CHAPTER 2
BREAKTHROUGH

❝ THOSE SUPPORTERS ARE UNBELIEVABLE. ❞

KEITH WOOD: It was a strange sequence of events. It started as a rumour. Actually, it was Charlie Mulqueen's doing. He wrote an article that I was thinking of coming back to Ireland – which was absolutely wrong. I hadn't the slightest intention of it. Next thing, Huw Morgan, the chief executive of Harlequins, asked to see me.

'It's come to my attention that you're thinking of going back to Ireland. We haven't heard anything about this.'

'It's not true.'

'But we saw it in the paper. Come on – are you thinking of going back?'

'No, I'm not, actually.'

'Well – would you like to go back?'

Huw's role was to shore up the finances and restructure the company. He went in there and he did what he needed to do. He pointed out that I was going to miss a lot of the season anyway, because the 1999 World Cup was coming up. He said: 'We're doing a restructuring here, so if you wanted to go for a year – and only a year – then we wouldn't stand in your way.'

So I said, 'OK, I'll have a chat with the union.' I knew I was basically being sent on loan. Sabbatical was the term we used at the time. It meant I had a chance to play for Munster. I had played in the 1994 season when we won the interpros for the first time in sixteen years. Part of the reason was to have a break because there was concern in the union about the number of games people were playing in England. The idea was that I wouldn't be jaded by the end of the year. As it turned out, I played more games than anybody in the country.

I loved it, for a variety of reasons. When I went over to Quins first I was blown away by their professionalism in comparison to Ireland. When I went back to Munster

WHEN I WENT BACK TO MUNSTER THERE WERE ELEMENTS STILL LACKING IN PROFESSIONALISM, BUT I WAS REALLY STRUCK BY THE CAMARADERIE AND THE JOKING CULTURE THAT IS MUNSTER.

there were elements still lacking in professionalism, but I was really struck by the camaraderie and the joking culture that is Munster. It was a stark contrast with anything in the UK. Part of that was because, if you grew up in Munster, you were going to play for Munster. So there was a unity of purpose that didn't exist in Quins. If you grew up in Twickenham, that didn't necessarily mean you were going to play for Quins. The guys who came in that year saw that this was something extraordinarily special.

Not long before I had played for Quins against Munster. We beat them at home and lost in Limerick. Quins were infinitely better on paper – better individual players – but we didn't have a better team. And that was the difference. That is the difference. Their sense of team is so much bigger than fifteen players. The supporters are part and parcel of it, and you get to know an awful lot of them by name.

JOHN KELLY: At the start of the season, we were all at the University of Limerick, and Dave Mahedy asking us to set our goals. What were our ambitions for the new season?

KILLIAN KEANE: Everyone does it now. But back then, it was all new to us. Nobody was saying anything. There was a bit of an embarrassed silence. Then Woody came out with it …

'Winning the Heineken Cup.'

JOHN KELLY: People started giggling. We couldn't believe what we'd just heard. It was the first time most of us had even thought about it.

KEITH WOOD: Being sensible is the key element of goal setting. The target has to be attainable. I remember doing one two or three years earlier with Quins. They said, 'Yeah – we're going to win everything.' And I said, 'That's bollocks. We don't have the team to win everything. Nor do we need to win everything.' There was a tournament at the time called the Anglo-Welsh League, and I remember saying, 'Who gives a shit whether we win the Anglo-Welsh League? We need to focus on the things that really matter to us as a club.' For Munster, it had to be the Heineken Cup. We had to set ourselves that target. If you looked around, you could see that team was actually capable of getting there and doing it. That day I felt we had to expose ourselves to the vulnerability that we're not mad about in Ireland – which is setting yourself up too high and then being knocked down.

There was a fear to mention it. There's a fine line between confidence and arrogance, and to state from the start that you're going to win the Heineken Cup means that you're going to be the best team in Europe, which means you are going to have some of the best players in Europe. And that lack of humility has never sat comfortably with Irish people. Never. I've always said that arrogance is a very important trait. You need to have some level of it. If you set your target to reach the final, you are almost guaranteeing that you'll lose it. If you set your target to win it, if you have the dream of holding the trophy at the end, then you have the chance of going out and doing the work to make that happen.

KILLIAN KEANE: At the time, everyone looked at Woody as if to say, 'What are you on about?' And the truth is that we were never going to win it until that moment. Not until somebody said, 'Well, why not?' None of us inside the system before that was going to come out with it because we were in a comfort zone. Drop the ball in training? Well, it happens. But Woody didn't see it that way. He said we were being paid, but we weren't professional. Not really. And he was right.

KEITH WOOD: I was cranky at that stage. I remember shoeing John Kelly because he fell over the ball in a ruck. I shoed the hell out of him. He said, 'What are you doing? *What are you doing?!*' And I said, 'If you did that in a match, it would be a penalty. And if you were the opposition in a match and you did it, I'd want to shoe you. So I'm going to do it to you in training. Just don't fall over the ball, OK?'

It was important that any criticism I put on to another player, I put on to myself. With the injuries I had, a lot of the time I couldn't train the way I would have liked. If I went too hard, my body would break down. So it became a balancing act for me, and that made it very hard for me to be properly critical, because there were things I just couldn't do myself. The only thing I could really guarantee was, 'Well, I'm not dropping a ball.' So I would say: 'You can't drop a ball in training. Why would you even contemplate finding that acceptable? You should be raging with yourself.'

Munster were a little bit easy on themselves, in training. On a Saturday, it was bodies-on-the-line stuff then – guaranteed. But ultimately, you play the way you train.

We beat Pontypridd at home in the first pool match and then came the big test: Saracens away. I knew we had a good team at that stage. We had good runners, a fairly solid scrum, we had a 9 who was very efficient at hitting his 10, a 10 who was pinging the ball into the corners at every opportunity. John Langford was brilliant in the lineout, and we were getting over the gain line easily. We were bloody aggressive, too.

When I played with Quins, if someone fell on the wrong side there would be a couple of guys who would ruck them out. Me, Jason Leonard and Bill Davison. That was it. In Munster, a centre would pass you out to give him a bit of a shoeing. It was an aggressive mindset and that counts for an awful lot. You had old heads, the Claw and Galwey, steeped in Munster. Instinctively, they knew what to do. And the next guy along was Foley – one of the smartest players I ever played with. There's a line called the Fat Man Track – the shortest distance between any two points, where the ball is or where it might end up. Foley instinctively knew that line and was there. Even though he wasn't faster than the other guys, he would beat them to the ball and once he got there he was incredibly effective.

I knew that beating Saracens on their pitch would be like flicking a chip off our shoulder. There was something about us. We had experience and we had potential, young guys coming through – Frankie Sheahan, Donncha O'Callaghan, Jeremy Staunton, Marcus Horan.

Peter Stringer is hauled back by Saracens captain François Pienaar, Vicarage Road, November 1999

MARCUS HORAN: Around the time Woody joined us I went up to Thomond Park for a chat with Declan Kidney. I was a student at the time, playing senior with Shannon, in the front row. When I got there, he just said, 'Look, we want to bring you on board with a development contract.' I nearly flew back to college to tell Kate, my girlfriend, now my wife. I just thought it was the best thing ever, to be contracted with Munster. Then I told my mates: 'Lads, I'm sorted for a job.'

Things happened really quickly. One of the biggest buzzes of my life was when I came on against Leinster in an interprovincial in Temple Hill. There was a scrum on our line. Everyone was a bit nervous about me coming in, because I wasn't the biggest guy at the time. I just had a feeling that guys weren't too sure about me. I put everything into that scrum, and it went well for us. I got a few pats on the back from some of the senior players after that. From then on, I was subbing for Claw. I felt like I belonged, you know? That I was part of it.

MICK GALWEY: That year some of us weren't picked for the World Cup squad. But Munster played Ireland in a warm-up match down in Musgrave Park and we beat them. We said, 'Hold on here. This is the Irish team that's going to the World Cup and we're after beating them.' By the month of September we had beaten Ireland and won the interpros and we had the time during World Cup to work on our fitness.

DECLAN KIDNEY: I went over to see Saracens before we played them and I couldn't believe all the ancillary stuff that was going on around their matches. They had a radio-controlled car bringing out the kicking tee, they had cheerleaders – girls that fellas could easily get distracted by – running out on to the pitch. There was pounding music after every score. It was all alien to Irish rugby at the time. And then they had supporters wearing their fez hats over at the side.

You always try to prepare the players, as much as you can, for what to expect. There's a little bar counter in Thomond Park, and in the run-up to the match I asked Niall O'Donovan to do the analysis while I bent down behind the bar counter. Next thing I stood up with a fez hat on me. My kids had radio-controlled cars – one of them fired cannonballs or something – so I started driving it around the place. And let's just say I covered the cheerleader angle as well. Niall kept presenting the stuff. After about three minutes I stopped the session.

'Right, tell me what happened there in the last three minutes. What was Niall saying?'

They couldn't tell me. So I said, 'Right lads – that's fourteen points that you'll be down.'

KILLIAN KEANE: That was the real start of the journey. No doubt about it. We played on a Sunday and we arrived on a Friday. Our preparation was getting better all the time.

MICK GALWEY: On the Saturday four of us went to see Watford play Sunderland at Vicarage Road, which was where Saracens played. That was our only chance to see the pitch. Niall Quinn was playing for Sunderland, and Alan Quinlan had met him once at the races. We were over by the side of the pitch, four Paddies, and Big Niall was kicking the ball around in the warm-up. Next thing Alan starts shouting over …

'Niall! Niall! Alan Quinlan here! Remember the time I met you at the races in Tipperary?'

'I do, yeah, I remember it well,' says Niall.

KILLIAN KEANE: Saracens were some team. They had François Pienaar, Richard Hill, Danny Grewcock, Scott Murray, Julian White, Thierry Lacroix … and they probably underestimated us.

Anthony Foley and Alan Quinlan celebrate victory over Saracens at Vicarage Road

GERRY THORNLEY, *THE IRISH TIMES*: Munster have had their days, the All Blacks and all that, but beating Saracens 35–34 at Vicarage Road yesterday in a pulsating Heineken European Cup tie was the best of the modern, professional era. For sheer character, it takes some beating. In eighty minutes they seemed to make more comebacks than Frank Sinatra, saving the best until last when coming back from 34–23 down in the last ten minutes. 'You've no idea how important it was,' said Keith Wood afterwards, even more ebullient than normal.

ANTHONY FOLEY: There weren't that many Munster supporters there, but there was still enough for your man to come over the loudspeaker system at the end and say it was it a public order offence to invade the pitch. But that still didn't stop them.

JOHN HAYES: A couple of weeks later we went to Colomiers and beat them, our first time winning in France. Jason Holland scored two tries that day. So the Saracens match at home became huge. It felt like there was 100,000 people at it. Fellas snuck it from everywhere. The official attendance was 14,000. It was in my arse. It was way more.

PETER STRINGER: Myself, Hayes and Rog all had big white bandages on our heads after being stitched. When Mick Galwey scored our first try I jumped up to celebrate, and David Wallace's two front teeth went into the top of my head. I can't remember anything after that.

MICK GALWEY: It was before the fire officer took any notice of Munster matches – they had to clamp down after that. We didn't play as well as we had over there, but with a few minutes to go we were leading by a point. Then Mark Mapletoft scored a try, and the crowd went silent. There wasn't a murmur out of them. Lacroix kicked the conversion, and we were six points down.

I pulled the boys together and said, 'Lads, we have to go back up there, we have to score. Our unbeaten record is on the line. Our season is on the line.' I probably didn't convince myself, but I might have convinced them.

KEITH WOOD: There wasn't even the hint of panic. It was, 'We'll break away up the field, keep going, and score.' And we said, 'Ah yeah. That's fair enough.' We all knew that was going to happen, and I think everybody else knew it was going to happen as well.

That, for me, was a turning point. A team losing in injury time, expecting to go up the field and score. Nobody was thinking, 'Oh, we're in trouble now.' A great level of trust had developed between the players for that to be the case.

MICK GALWEY: I remember the plays, Mikey Mullins taking on balls and the penalty being given. We did like we always did – kicked to the corner. Our bread and butter ball was on Langford. He went up in the middle of the lineout, we cleaned it, drove on a bit, cleared a few rucks and if there was ever a poacher for a try near the line, it was Woody.

Jason Holland dives for the line in the return match against Saracens at Thomond Park, January 2000

KEITH WOOD: I had to score it, because it was my fault they had scored the previous one. I missed a tackle, so I owed them one. Ronan had the conversion then to win it 31–30, and I couldn't watch.

RONAN O'GARA: I put the ball down and I starting thinking about what had happened to David Humphreys the previous year. He'd missed a penalty that would have beaten France. I lined it up again. I had to get a positive thought into my mind. Then I thought, 'Relax – this is going over.'

Above and opposite: **Stand up and fight: John Langford and Mick Galwey celebrate the one-point win over Saracens**

The Saracens players charged at O'Gara before he had made contact with the ball. To some in the ground it looked like he had missed, that the ball was heading fractionally wide, but then it struck an upright and bounced in.

When the players reached their dressing room, after finally being released from the embrace of their delirious supporters, they broke open bottles of champagne and sang a song they had first heard four months before during a sing-song in Belfast, where they had beaten Ulster for the first time in two decades. The song was a favourite of Brian O'Brien, the team manager. As a selector of the Munster team that beat the All Blacks in 1978, he had blasted it out on a short tour to London shortly before that unforgettable day. The song was called 'Stand Up And Fight' and it would become the anthem of the modern Munster team.

Stand up and fight until you hear the bell,
Stand toe to toe, trade blow for blow,
Keep punching till you make your punches tell,
Show that crowd what you know!
Until you hear that bell, that final bell,
Stand up and fight like hell!

'Wow,' said the millionaire owner of Saracens, Nigel Wray, of the mayhem all around him. 'If you have to lose, then let it be in an atmosphere like that. Those supporters are unbelievable.'

O'Gara, who had also landed a last-minute kick to beat Saracens at Vicarage Road, was circumspect in the moment of glory. 'I'm two for two in these situations, but there will be a time when it doesn't go over,' he said.

Six weeks later, in February 2000, O'Gara, Stringer and Hayes were capped by Ireland. In April, Stade Français came to Thomond Park for the quarter-final and were beaten 27–10. O'Gara kicked seventeen points, and Dominic Crotty and Anthony

Horgan scored a try apiece. Many of the Munster players were over at Anthony Foley's house in Killaloe when news came of the draw for the semi-finals. The four teams left standing were Munster, Llanelli, Northampton and Toulouse. Everyone knew what the coffin draw was: Toulouse, away.

The players stood around a radio and heard Munster's fate being read out. Toulouse. Away.

MICK GALWEY: On the Monday before training, Declan pulled us together and said, 'This was the draw we wanted.' Typical Declan. Convincing us that we really wanted to play Toulouse in France.

For some of us, the previous hiding was on our minds, 60–19. To make matters worse, Ireland had just beaten France in Paris, and the Toulouse players were thinking, 'This is our chance to get back at the Irish.' That blew our cover: as if they needed extra motivation.

DECLAN KIDNEY: The match was in Bordeaux. When we got to the ground all their supporters were already there. There were 3,000 Munster fans in the ground, but I said, 'Sure we might as well warm up in front of their supporters.' They roared and shouted and for fifteen minutes we couldn't hear a thing. At the end I told them, 'That's about as loud as it's going to get and ye are still alive. As you can see, it has no effect on ye. All ye have to worry about now is dealing with the fellas coming out to face ye in a while.'

BARRY MURPHY: I was doing my Leaving Cert about three weeks later, but there was no way I was missing that. Myself, my older brother and my father went over. We were behind one goal with some other lads from school. I didn't even know they were going – it was the biggest crowd ever to follow Munster away, by far. We all stood up from our seats – it was best atmosphere ever. Did I think it might be me out there one day? Never for a minute. I didn't think I was anywhere near good enough.

ANTHONY FOLEY: I jarred my back the week of the match. I spent most of the time lying on the ground in the run-up to it. I was wearing a corset and in the pre-match photo

ON THE MONDAY BEFORE TRAINING, DECLAN PULLED US TOGETHER AND SAID, 'THIS WAS THE DRAW WE WANTED.' TYPICAL DECLAN. CONVINCING US THAT WE REALLY WANTED TO PLAY TOULOUSE IN FRANCE.

A hot summer day in the south of France: Eddie Halvey breaks away against Toulouse in the Heineken Cup semi-final, May 2000

I looked like I'd been eating pork pies and drinking a gallon of Guinness. It was a hot summer's day in the south of France, and Toulouse were coming to hockey us.

KEITH WOOD: In the first half I made a break and hilariously outstripped Emile Ntamack. He eventually caught me and tackled me, and I tore my calf. I knew it was pretty bad but I played on for the rest of the half. We were doing well. John Hayes scored a try for us, and we were only a few points down at half-time.

ANTHONY FOLEY: Coming in at half-time it was an uphill walk all the way to the changing rooms, about 500 metres and we felt every one of them. We were knackered by the time we got there.

DECLAN KIDNEY: The heat was unreal. Toulouse just came as far as the tunnel and sat down. So our lads walked over them and saw how wrecked they were. Ian Fleming had all the towels in ice. They put them around their legs, their backs, their heads.

KEITH WOOD: We tried to strap up my calf, but I was really struggling. Coming back out they had gone about 40 yards in front of me, and I couldn't keep up with them. So I was shouting after them, 'Put Frankie on!' Frankie Sheahan had a bloody excellent half. We bullied the hell out of them. We won – and we won quite comfortably.

RONAN O'GARA: After about sixty minutes we were outside our twenty-two and I threw a miss pass to Mikey Mullins. He ran on and switched to Dominic Crotty. Jason Holland got involved, John Kelly, Axel, Strings, Hoggy [Anthony Horgan], practically the whole team. Then Dominic ran a great line and took two of them out, and I was screaming for the pass. He just popped it up to me, and I was clean through under the sticks. I did this silly celebration and starting punching the air to the Munster people. It was the best try I ever scored.

DECLAN KIDNEY: Dutchy [Jason Holland] scored an intercept try after that – there was a fella using the analysis, a guy who had done his homework. He took a potshot and it paid off.

Keith Wood, Mick Galwey and Peter Clohessy

The dressing room at Toulouse: Frankie Sheahan, left, with Keith Wood, for whom he came on as a sub

DOMINIC CROTTY: Before the Toulouse match we received hundreds of lovely faxes, congratulating us on our season. It was real 'thanks for the memories' stuff. Nobody believed we could win – apart from ourselves. For the next three weeks I woke up every morning with thoughts of the final in my head. There was no escape. I'll never forget seeing small children in their pyjamas waiting for us in Shannon airport on the Saturday night after we beat Toulouse.

DECLAN KIDNEY: Back then we didn't own a scrummaging machine. We used to borrow the one out at the university, but they had moved it because the season was over. So before playing Northampton in the final we had to go out to Annacotty to do some scrummaging. We hadn't been able to do much because Woody was injured and Peter Clohessy was wrecked. When they hit the machine it had rusted, so it didn't hold them. There was a fella there with a tractor, cutting the grass, so we put his tractor at one end of the machine and scrummaged at the other end of it. That wasn't anybody's fault. It was just the evolution of professionalism.

DAVID WALLACE: Northampton had a lot of injuries going into the game. I remember talking to Paul, my brother, and he really thought we could do it. Maybe we got a bit complacent, I don't know. But for us the final became less of a match and more of an occasion.

KEITH WOOD: We got things wrong before the final. On the Friday we ended up getting caught in traffic going to the ground and coming back. We tried to do too many things that we felt should be done. We were playing the match in our heads too much beforehand so by the time we got to it we were very edgy. There's a technical term for it, a psychological term – over-arousal. We got to the point where we were too excited. That was often the way in Ireland, because we had to be like that – boot, bite and bollock and all that. But there comes a point then where it's very hard to get your balance back. We weren't in the place where we should have been. Then we had a meeting the night before the match, and it tipped us over the edge.

MICK GALWEY: I didn't do it intentionally – I was just trying to do what I thought was right. But it took on a life of its own. At the meeting that night I said, 'What does it mean to you to be here?' I wanted a reaction from a few players. Then all of a sudden it starting going around the room and it got very emotional, to say the least.

DECLAN KIDNEY: In hindsight that meeting was a problem, but there was nothing you could do at the time. It's just another one of those experience things. You could look upon it as a terrible meeting or you could look upon it as the most powerful meeting you were ever at. You could say it was hugely inspiring, or hugely draining. Maybe it should have been curtailed earlier on, or maybe it was just something that needed to be done. To have stepped in would not have been appropriate. I had to wait for the door to be opened. When the moment came I said, 'Right, that's OK now.'

PETER STRINGER: For me it was a very strange, eerie feeling. There were already masses of faxes on the wall, and that was fair enough. We knew what it meant to the supporters, or we thought we did anyway. But when you see your own team-mates, the guys you look up to, bawling their eyes out – that brings so much pressure on you as a young player. They were saying, 'This is it, lads, this will be the greatest day of our lives.' They were building it up and building it up, and I was thinking, 'Jesus, what is this about? This isn't what I thought rugby was going to be like when I was a kid. I didn't sign up for this when I signed my contract.' I'll never forget how horrible I felt coming out of that room, the sick feeling in my stomach.

David Wallace celebrates scoring the only try of the 2000 Heineken Cup final, against Northampton, with Anthony Horgan

KEITH WOOD: Northampton were clinical, they were hard and they were aggressive. They didn't make any mistakes. Wally scored the only try of the match, and they didn't do anything of any note – they just played very hard, heavy rugby. We only lost 9–8 but we couldn't argue.

DAVID WALLACE: You can't blame Rog for what happened. We shouldn't have needed a penalty to win in the last minute. The game is played over eighty minutes. If we were going to win it, we should have won it before then. It shouldn't have come down to one kick.

RONAN O'GARA: I lined it up – it was over on the left hand side, the side I prefer to kick from. I hit it pretty well, but it just ran out of pace really and the wind dragged it a bit. It didn't miss by very much – but that doesn't really matter. It missed.

Hard, heavy rugby: Keith Wood

MICK GALWEY: At the final whistle we were all devastated, but Declan said, 'Come on, we need to thank the supporters.' Then they started singing and rising to their feet. If they had stood up and started booing it might have been easier. We felt we had let them down. The younger players were especially upset. Then my wife Joan handed me my little girl, Neasa, and I broke down. It was hard to take. I was still in a state of shock.

It had been some trip, though. I remember coming off the pitch in Toulouse and somebody handed me a phone. He said, 'There's a man here wants to talk to you – Richard.'

I said, 'Who the fuck is Richard?' But I took the phone anyway.

'How're you doing, Micky? This is Dicky here. Dicky Harris. I'm calling you from Mexico!'

Opposite: 'It didn't miss by very much – but that doesn't really matter. It missed.'

An emotional Mick Galwey with his daughter, Neasa

'Jaysus, 'tis yourself.'

'Well done – what a win! Fantastic! I'm proud of you all! And I have to go to the final! No matter where I am in the world or what I'm doing, I'm going to be at that final. Would you mind if I came?'

'Of course you can come, Dicky – of course you can!'

At the time he was regarded as a bit of a Jonah. He was a Young Munster supporter, and every time he went to see them, they would lose. I was thinking, 'Jesus, nobody will even know he's there.' We were inside in the dressing room after the match and who walks in only Richard Harris and Peter O'Toole. Peter Clohessy looked up and said, 'What the fuck is *he* doing here?'

PETER STRINGER: It's weird – I have almost no recollection of it. All I can remember is seeing a documentary afterwards. Some of it was in black and white, they had slow-motion shots of Gaillimh crying and holding his little girl. The background music was 'Fields Of Gold', by Sting. Every time I hear that bloody song I think of it.

KEITH WOOD: Ultimately, that set the standard. When we had set our goals at the start, I don't know how many people in that room believed we could actually win it. There's a difference between saying it and believing it. But now they could see: 'Yes, we can do that. Because we've just come within kicking distance of it.' It was a journey for the psyche.

The end of the match was one of the worst feelings I've ever had – and it was one of the highlights of my career. Within thirty seconds of the final whistle, the whole 40,000 Munster supporters started singing. It was the best display of empathy I have ever experienced, the most extraordinary, spontaneous response. I thought it was startling. For the simple reason that you had 40,000 people there who said, 'Yeah, you've lost, and you didn't play as well as you could have or should have – but we thank you for it anyway. And we are with you.' That day, the bond between the supporters and the team was forged. The deal was that they would get to the end of the road together. That they would get that trophy.

> **THE END OF THE MATCH WAS ONE OF THE WORST FEELINGS I'VE EVER HAD — AND IT WAS ONE OF THE HIGHLIGHTS OF MY CAREER. WITHIN THIRTY SECONDS OF THE FINAL WHISTLE, THE WHOLE 40,000 MUNSTER SUPPORTERS STARTED SINGING. IT WAS THE BEST DISPLAY OF EMPATHY I HAVE EVER EXPERIENCED, THE MOST EXTRAORDINARY, SPONTANEOUS RESPONSE.**

CHAPTER 3
RONAN O'GARA'S STORY

❝ I'M AN ORDINARY BLOKE WHO'S WORKED HARD AT HIS JOB. ❞

A while after the Northampton match I was in a bar with a few of the boys. I went to go to the bathroom, and this guy was smirking at me. Then he said, 'How do I know you?'

'I don't know …'

'Oh yeah, I remember. You're the wanker that missed the kick against Northampton.'

An isolated incident. Mostly people are wonderful. There's an amazing amount of goodwill out there. But I don't have a problem if someone says something that isn't nice. You'll always get people like that. I've put myself in this position, and it comes with the responsibility I feel for what I do. I can handle it. It's fine.

Confidence comes with experience. My goal-kicking technique in those days wasn't anywhere near as developed as it is now. I suppose I've always had an ability to kick the ball, ever since I was a kid, but back then it was a case of '*please* go over …'

I have a great life, and great friends. I'm an ordinary bloke who's worked hard at his job. That's the thing that motivates me. I've seen where I can get with hard work and – I believe – a good gift from God.

I don't think I'd be where I am today without Jonny Wilkinson. He has set standards for players in our position. On the 2001 Lions tour I saw his work ethic first-hand and I tapped into that. You've got to want to be the best in the world. I admire the man as a person too, the way he has dealt with things, all the stuff he's had to put up with.

I'm not that comfortable with the attention either, to be honest. It's not in my character to revel in it. I'm pretty low-key. I don't really do the fancy stuff – I don't wear jewellery or drive a fast car or have hip-hop blaring or go around flashing myself here, there and everywhere. I wouldn't say my personality has changed at all, over the years. In this job, you've got to try to keep yourself stable or you become impossible to live with. Some weeks are harder than others, though.

Some fellas can breeze the build-up to big games. I can't – I have to be focused. I have to do my mental preparation, I have to I feel that I'm ready. I don't want to be putting myself out there for credit, but I have a big impact on how Munster perform. When it's coming up to a big match, rugby is the only thing in my head. Driving around, I visualize certain scenarios, different positions on the pitch, different times when the ball is coming to me.

Starting off, I would have been pretty nervous going into matches. I don't want to sound cocky but I feel that, in my position, I probably have the most influence on the game. That means a lot to me.

My mum was always telling me that you get out of life what you put into it, and that stuck in my head. There are a lot of stupid expressions out there, but I like that one. You've got to do things the right way in your job, you've got to be totally honest. That's one trait none of us in the Munster squad is shy on.

If you're honest with people it can never come back to bite you. If you speak your mind freely, then you don't have any tracks to cover. I've seen an awful lot of people who talk bullshit and are two-faced. I won't accept that. If there's an issue then I confront it. Maybe I didn't always have the self-confidence to do that, but that's just part of growing as a person.

My first steps in rugby were with the Under-8s at Cork Con and up through the ranks there and at my school, Pres. I always played out-half; I just liked the fact that you get so much of the ball. My dad played for Connacht, so we knew the game. He was always pushing out the next challenge for me, getting me to set my standards high. There were times when I didn't want to hear the advice he was giving me, but it always turned out that he was right. Any time he felt I was getting a bit above myself, he'd tell me – in a nice way.

When I first started playing for Munster, there were guys like Mick Galwey and Peter Clohessy around, and you had to prove yourself as a player before you got their respect. As a person, too.

> **I ALWAYS PLAYED OUT-HALF; I JUST LIKED THE FACT THAT YOU GET SO MUCH OF THE BALL. MY DAD PLAYED FOR CONNACHT, SO WE KNEW THE GAME. HE WAS ALWAYS PUSHING OUT THE NEXT CHALLENGE FOR ME, GETTING ME TO SET MY STANDARDS HIGH.**

If I had a penalty and I kicked it, Galwey would say 'Good man, Rog.' Hearing that used to give me a big boost. I don't get that these days, I suppose because I'm a senior player now.

For me the game is about instinct – your ability to read situations, to implement decisions very quickly and accurately, to perform under pressure. My game is about finding space and putting people into it, about thinking two or three phases ahead. Sometimes we're not all on the same wavelength, but that's another improvement we can make as a team.

I always want to be the best player on the team – simple as that. That's the standard I set for myself. Mediocrity doesn't sit well with me, and that's why I have huge time for someone like Paul O'Connell. He's a born winner, incredibly driven. Sometimes people might think he's a bit harsh, that he looks for too much, but I'd back him 100 per cent. We have to ask ourselves the hard questions.

Looking back at that penalty against Northampton, I was happy with the kick because it was difficult – but not with the outcome, of course. I'm a better player now, and if I had it again in the last minute of a final I'd expect to kick it.

Sport does that to you. It might seem like the end of the world, for a little while. But you get on with it. You know there will be other days, other kicks.

CHAPTER 4
EMPTY-HANDED AGAIN

❝ THIS CAUSE HAS COME SO FAR NOW, THERE'S NO TURNING BACK. ❞

On the day the draw was made for the Heineken European Cup of 2000–2001, the rugby journalists of Europe asked themselves an obligatory question: which was the pool of death? They settled on Pool 4: Bath, Castres, Munster, Newport. By now the tournament was a stunning success. In five years it had produced a string of classic matches, epic occasions that outstripped most internationals for quality, intensity and, above all, emotion. Five teams had put their names on the cup: Toulouse, Brive, Bath, Ulster and Northampton. Munster had contributed as much as any of those champions in putting the tournament where it now stood, but as the new season dawned the bookmakers were dismissive of their chances of climbing the mountain once more. They were 20–1 to win it. But if that was an insult, it was not an unwelcome one. The more they were written off, the better they liked it.

They were bang in form, too, newly crowned as interprovincial champions for the third year running. Over two seasons they had won nineteen of their twenty-one matches in all competitions. Once again they were led by the galvanizing Mick Galwey, who had just become the first player to win 100 Munster caps. First up, at their Thomond Park bearpit, were Newport – bolstered by the arrival of a string of luminaries such as the former Springbok captain Gary Teichmann. Among the Munster faithful, expectations had soared – a situation which did not necessarily sit comfortably with Declan Kidney, the coach. 'They're as strong as Saracens last year,' Kidney said of Newport. 'Tell me where they're weaker?'

Munster won, but they were hard pressed, and the only thing anyone in the camp was feeling at the end of a 26–18 victory was relief. The players were slumped in their dressing room after it and they took some convincing before they allowed themselves to enjoy the moment with a sing-song. When they went to Castres the following week and came from 20–6 down to win 32–29, Kidney put his finger on the vulnerability that was now helping to drive them on: 'This year what I admire so much is that they know the hurt that could be ahead of them and yet they're still willing to say, "Right, let's put ourselves out there and see what happens."'

Seven days later Bath came to a raucous Thomond Park and were hammered 31–9, their worst defeat in Europe. 'I can see now how Munster got to the final last season,' said their coach, John Hall. Such clarity of thought after a Thomond Park drubbing would become a recurring theme for the coaches of English clubs trying to end Munster's unbeaten record at home. They had to experience it for themselves before they could begin understand the forces they were up against.

On they went, into the quarter-final, with a home draw against Biarritz. Nobody could see the French team tearing up the script, but they went close. Maybe Munster were nervous, maybe they tightened up as the big prize came into view again, but they were not themselves that Sunday afternoon. They came through 38–29 thanks to some big individual performances: Alan Quinlan, Ronan O'Gara and the unyielding Anthony Foley, who scored three tries.

Cruelly, and for the second year running, Munster were drawn away in France in the semi-final. Taking on Stade Français was always going to be difficult, but restrictions put in place to keep foot-and-mouth disease out of Ireland had caused the cancellation of matches and meant Munster travelled to Lille badly short of game time. Quinlan had broken his thumb, and the inexperienced lock Donncha O'Callaghan was called into the back row. As the match day dawned, Foley made a confession to the press. 'The wounds from last year have started to open again,' he said. 'The hurt is starting to come back. You look at the score, 9–8, and think, jeez, one kick.'

Lille, however, was to bring more heartbreak – as well as enduring controversy. In front of 8,000 of their fanatical supporters, a Munster team that was never really firing went down 16–15: another single-point sickener. The match will forever be remembered for a try by John O'Neill twelve minutes into the second half, a legitimate score not given.

JOHN O'NEILL: The ball bounced nicely for me, I went towards the corner flag and got the ball down. No doubt about it. I think if I'd gone in lower the linesman [Steve Lander]

Opposite top: Mick Galwey leads the side out to face Stade Français for the semi-final in Lille, April 2001 Opposite bottom: John O'Neill touches down, but the try was disallowed

would have seen it. But I went in high and put it down in the corner. I rolled over, certain that I'd scored. I even looked at Dominici and the rest of the Stade Français boys. They all thought it was a try. I was absolutely sure it would be given. Then I looked at the linesman, and he looked at the referee. Out of a fifty-fifty call, they decided it wasn't a try.

MICK GALWEY: Straight away I told them, 'You've got to go to the video ref!' They told me they couldn't – there wasn't one. To lose by a point two years in a row was devastating. Afterwards one of the lads said, 'It would be great to get a hiding some time.'

RONAN O'GARA: It could have been a point, it could have been twenty. It doesn't make a difference, we lost. Maybe it would be better if it was twenty, because at least we could then say we were beaten by a better side. I don't think anybody inside in our dressing room thought they were a better side. But we didn't do our talking on the pitch. We just didn't perform.

DONNCHA O'CALLAGHAN: I found out two days before that I was starting. Afterwards I thought holding up my hand was the right thing to do when I'd played like a bag of shite. That's the way we do things in Munster – we go behind the posts, and if you're at fault you put your hand up. At the time I felt like I'd let people down. I've watched that video since and, while I did make some mistakes, I didn't play that badly. But I was young and maybe a bit too honest. Later on I made a big thing out of it to journalists – how bad I felt in the dressing room afterwards, thinking I'd let the lads down. In one way I'm disappointed I did that – I could have just said nothing and nobody would have been any the wiser. But, in another way, it really stood to me.

DECLAN KIDNEY: Donncha made one or two mistakes but because he was a younger guy played out of position, his errors were highlighted more than other fellas'. That's the world we live in. Sometimes you have to go through things like that to test yourself.

The lads went on a lap of honour at the end of that match. In lots of ways you wouldn't feel like doing it, but there was absolutely no question that we were going to. It was the only way that we could thank our people, to recognize the effort and expense they'd gone to in being there.

John Langford on the rueful lap of honour after the one-point semi-final defeat to Stade Français in 2001

Jim Williams was thirty-two by the time he joined Munster a few months later in the summer of 2001, but he had plenty left in the tank. A back-row warrior with the ACT Brumbies in Super 12, he had only begun playing top-class rugby at the age of twenty-nine. It broke his heart when – after winning fouteen caps for Australia – he was overlooked for the visit of the Lions that summer. If he felt bitter about how his career in Australia ended, that would have suited Munster just fine. People with a point to prove always fitted right in there.

Williams had been told good things about Munster by the departing Australian John Langford, and he was not the only big-name addition to the squad. Rob Henderson, an impressive performer for the Lions in Australia, joined from Wasps. In August, a third new player made his debut in a pre-season friendly against Bath, a towering 21-year-old lock from Young Munster. Unknown then, but not for long.

PAUL O'CONNELL: I couldn't believe I was in a dressing room with these guys. It was only earlier that year that I'd hopped over the wall to get into the match against Biarritz. What you do when you're hopping the wall is you leave a few of the young fellas off first. They go one way and get chased; you go the other way.

ROB HENDERSON: I'd come to the end of my contract at Wasps, and there was a World Cup coming up in 2003. I seriously wanted to play in it. It had been intimated that they [the IRFU] wanted the players back in Ireland – which for me wasn't a problem. Wasps offered me another contract, for more money, but I turned it down flat to come and be part of it at Munster.

That year we had Castres, Harlequins and Bridgend in the group stage. We qualified from that but got an away draw in the quarter-final, at Stade Français. We were staying in this big, tall hotel in the middle of Paris. Normally there's a card school – a few hands in the evening to kill the time. We were eight floors up, it was incredibly hot in the room, the air conditioning wasn't working and we couldn't open the windows, so we were sitting there practically naked – it was like a game of strip poker. That night the old adage 'one more hand' kept getting trotted out until eventually we called it quits. I could get people in trouble here, so I'd better not mention it was me, Mick O'Driscoll and Wally. I can't say who won either – but the conservatory's looking great, Wally.

We were training at the stadium the day before and there was this guy there who looked a bit suspicious, so our press officer, Pat Geraghty, was sent over to him because he allegedly had some French. Pat went over but the guy kept saying, 'comprend pas, comprend pas'. So Pat said, 'OK, then, vous comprendez fuck off?'

PAT GERAGHTY: We were meant to have the stadium to ourselves, but when the lads were doing lineouts there was this guy watching and talking into a mobile phone. Claw shouted over to me, 'Gerty, tell yer man to fuck off with himself.' It was only my second season, so whatever the Claw asked me to do, I was going to do it. I went down and asked him to leave, but he stayed where he was. I grabbed his phone and walked away with it. There was a little argy-bargy then and a punch was thrown. On the way back to the hotel the lads were singing the theme song from *Rocky*. Mick Galwey referred to it the next day. He said Geraghty had shown we weren't going to take any shit from the French.

Opposite: **Stade Français again: Paul O'Connell gets huge elevation in the quarter-final in Paris, January 2002**

Pat Geraghty with Peter Stringer after the final whistle

ROB HENDERSON: Poor fella – he was only cleaning the seats. We battled in that match. We went 16–3 up before half-time and never scored another point. But we hung on.

DENIS WALSH, *THE SUNDAY TIMES*: They dredged victory from the pit of their stomachs and the bottom of their hearts. For fifteen breathless minutes they stuck fast to the cliff's edge, clinging to a two-point lead when all Stade Français needed was a penalty from anywhere within 50 metres of the Munster posts. Only their discipline matched their endurance. For close on ninety minutes they tackled with unbending ferocity and sacrifice. On a terrible pitch and in a gusting, swirling wind, the premium on control was huge. Both teams struggled terribly in the lineout, but Paul O'Connell stood up and made a fist of it. An Ireland career awaits him, nothing surer.

ANTHONY FOLEY: We played as a unit. Everyone stepped forward and did what was required. We put up with the sly punches, the sly digs. We kept our cool, focused on what we wanted to achieve and produced our best performance for a long time.

ALAN QUINLAN: It's not mentioned that often, but that was a magnificent win. Paul O'Connell was man of the match. He'd only broken into the team, and we slaughtered him over the interview he gave on TV afterwards.

'Well done, Paul – that was some performance by Munster. A famous victory!'

'It was unreal!'

'And what about those wonderful supporters, Paul – what have you got to say about them?'

'They were unreal!'

'Well congratulations, Paul – you've been voted man of the match today. How does that feel?'

'Unreal!'

ROB HENDERSON: We got another away draw in France for the semi-final, about three months later. Another expensive trip for the supporters. And at one stage it looked like we were going to have to go there without Claw.

PETER CLOHESSY: I was burning rubbish in my garden and I had poured some petrol on the fire, but when I lit some paper there was some more petrol between me and the fire. All of a sudden the flames just shot up at me. I kept my eyes closed but I remember being able to smell my hair burn as I rolled around on the ground to put out the flames. Everybody else was inside in the house, and nobody realized what had happened until it was all over. I thought that was it, to be honest. I thought my career was finished.

MICK GALWEY: It would have been a terrible way to go out. But you knew that if there was any chance of him making it, he was going to be in Béziers. And sure enough, he was.

ROB HENDERSON: Deccie's big thing back then was *The Lion King*. When we were driving to the ground for the semi-final he had it on in the coach. He liked the scene where the monkey hits the lion over the head with a stick. The lion says, 'Ow! What was that for?' And the monkey goes, 'It doesn't matter, it's in the past. The past can hurt – but you can either run from it, or learn from it.' All that carry-on. And I'm like, 'Deccie, we're about to play the semi-final of the European Cup and we're watching *The Lion King* – you need serious help!' But whatever he does, it seems to work. So fair play.

DONNCHA O'CALLAGHAN: That match was huge for me. I came on for Axel early in the first half and I knew I had to deliver this time. Then I had to come off again because Claw was sin-binned and I vividly remember sitting down for those ten minutes and having a bit of a chat with myself. I was saying, 'You've got to show them. You've got to show them you're not unworthy of their expectations.' There are games in your career where you can settle people's nerves about you, where you can show them they don't have to have doubts about you. And that was the game for me.

DECLAN KIDNEY: Donners came on and had a huge impact. I don't know if we would have won that game without him – and I wouldn't usually say things like that.

ROB HENDERSON: Rags [John Kelly] scored the winning try in the last minute. Mr Reliable. I don't know why they call him Rags, because I've never seen him grumpy. The next day we found out we'd be playing Leicester in the final. One to go.

John Kelly, scorer of the winning try in the 2002 semi-final against Castres

MICK GALWEY: Getting back there was huge, it proved we weren't a flash in the pan. We were coming up against English opposition again and we knew they were a better side than Northampton. Everyone of us who had been there in 2000 was saying, 'Look we screwed up the last time, let's learn from that.' We changed things around – and then on the day we were beaten by a better team.

ROB HENDERSON: The atmosphere that day was incredible. I never thought it would be beaten. You're playing against a Leicester team that everyone wants to beat. Full of stars. The previous final was still quite raw in a lot of the players' minds. When you get to that stage it's all about trying to score tries. If you get even one on the board, it makes a hell of a difference. You need to score a try and maybe we didn't quite have the ambition. We were happy to soak up and kick the threes. Play the territory and play that grinding forward game that we know works so well against any team in Europe. And that counted against us.

PETER O'REILLY, *SUNDAY TRIBUNE*: Munster's supporters will cite Neil Back's professional foul as the difference, coming as it did in the final minute when Munster were throwing body and soul at Leicester. But this is misguided. The key element was that Leicester could soak it all up and respond. When they needed to, Leicester produced two rapier thrusts that ultimately proved fatal. We wuz robbed? Sorry, lads, but no.

RONAN O'GARA: People go on about Neil Back's hand in the lineout, but he's a good player, he fooled the ref and fair play to him. If one of our lads had done it, he'd have been a legend. Neil Back wasn't the reason we didn't win the European Cup. The reason was because we didn't score any tries.

ALAN QUINLAN: I'm not sure if we really believed, deep down, that we could win it. We were really determined and highly charged, and at the time we probably believed we could win it. But not enough. They had so many experienced internationals and they had their homework done on us. They caught us in a few lineouts and their game plan was better. We thought we had learned, but we hadn't. We weren't good enough.

Opposite: Celebrating Munster's return to the Heineken Cup final after the
semi-final win over Castres: (top) Jerry Holland, Niall O'Donovan and Declan Kidney;
(middle) Rob Henderson and Peter Clohessy; (bottom) Ronan O'Gara

PETER STRINGER: I remember bending down to put the ball in the scrum and next thing it was gone. It turned to the touch judge. In my head I was like, 'Did you not *see* that?' And he was standing there with his hands behind his back, no flag out or anything. Afterwards I used to play the move out in my mind – he wouldn't knock the ball out of my hands and we'd score under the posts. Then I'd be thinking, 'Shit, that actually didn't happen.' He got away with it. That happens in rugby.

ANTHONY FOLEY: Anthony Horgan had broken his finger in the training run-out the day before. Freak accident, but you begin to wonder whether it's ever going to happen for us. It was Deccie and Niall's last game. They were joining the Ireland coaching staff, and afterwards it was all very emotional, one of those sad moments. If we'd had a trophy in the dressing room it would have felt feel like they had completed the job. But it wasn't to be. And we knew we had to keep plugging away. We had to keep putting our hat in the ring.

DECLAN KIDNEY: Losing the two finals was hugely disappointing. But I don't see those teams as failures. I see those as hugely successful teams. Because I know where we were coming from.

MICK GALWEY: After a defeat like that, two things are always hard. Getting off the plane and facing the people back in Shannon was tough. And then the press conference straight afterwards. You had to be professional and answer the questions thrown to you. I remember saying, 'Look, Munster will win the Heineken Cup one day – I really believe that. People like me mightn't be around, but this cause has come so far now, there's no turning back.' I knew I was going to be stepping aside as captain. I'd been on the road a long time and it was time to let the younger guys come through.

When I came into the team I got the Number 4 jersey that Moss Keane and Donal Lenihan wore before me. I passed it on to Donncha O'Callaghan. It's a special thing. You are playing for the jersey and what it represents – and what it represents is what's good in people, in Munster people. Fair enough, we hadn't won the cup and that was hard for me to take. It was for all of us. But people all over the world had seen what that jersey means to us.

Opposite top: Munster players collapse with disappointment at the final whistle of the 2002 Heineken Cup final Opposite bottom: Neasa Galwey joins her father and his team-mates in a dejected trudge past the trophy that had eluded them again

CHAPTER 5
PETER STRINGER'S STORY

❝ THIS IS WHAT I KNOW. ❞

I got a letter from England a while after the Leicester final and before I started reading it I looked at the bottom to see who it was from. It said, 'Best wishes, Neil Back'. I was thinking, 'Jesus, is he apologizing or something?'

It was all about his testimonial year the following season. I wasn't sure why he was writing to me about it. Then there was a line at the end – 'Would you write something in my testimonial book about your experiences in the Heineken Cup final? Here's my mobile number. Give me a shout.' It didn't hit me as being a very genuine letter. Maybe if there had been another mention of it earlier, if it hadn't read like he had printed off almost the same letter and sent it to a hundred other fellows. I didn't do anything about it in the end. I don't know whether that was right or wrong; it was just the way I felt at the time. But I don't have any bad feelings about Neil Back. What happened that day is forgotten about, it's in the past.

I've always seen myself as being a fighter. I don't think I'll ever be built up to something as a rugby player. It's been like that for me since I was seven years of age, and I've learned how to cope with it. When I was a boy people would say I was too small to play rugby. I'd get looks from the opposition, fellas saying, 'What's this guy doing here? Is he for real? The size of him!' Comments like that are still in my head. It was only when I was older that I found it was coming from other parents, too. They were saying to my mother and father, 'You're not going to let him play rugby, are you?'

I think you can see from boys' reactions when they start out playing rugby if they're able for it or not. If my parents had had any doubts at all they would have stopped me playing the game. But I loved it so much. I got such a kick out of standing out, I suppose because I was so much smaller than everyone else. I have videos at home of under-8 matches and I can't believe the things I see myself doing. It's like I had less fear then than I do now.

My dad, Johnny, was a member of Dolphin, and there would always be rugby balls around the place – real heavy leather ones full of water and hard to pick up. When I was five or six he'd be standing in the middle of the garden and he'd have me running around and passing the ball to him. I think he could see then that I wasn't going to be able to play anywhere else but scrum-half. He came up with some drills for me to practise in the garden, but he never put any pressure on me. He just said to enjoy it.

I went to school at Pres. Declan Kidney was a teacher there and he became a mentor for me – a rugby mentor. He lived and breathed the game, and it was the same for me. It felt like best thing in the world when teachers and friends respected you for your ability to play rugby. When I was in sixth year I went off on my own swimming twice a week for fifty minutes non-stop, because I wanted to develop upper-body strength for going into tackles. I was never going to be at a level where I could compete against much bigger guys one to one, and the margins in which I was able to improve physically were small, but I still had to work as hard as I possibly could at it. I was always told that if you take them by the ankles they're going to hit the ground, no matter how big they are. I had to go into games knowing I'd done as much as I could to be physically right.

I think I've done OK. There's a photograph on my wall at home. A friend of mine had it framed for me. It's from the match against Saracens in 1999, the first one. It shows me being dragged to the ground by François Pienaar, the World Cup-winning captain (*see page 49*). He looks huge in the photograph, compared with me. I was just a year into my professional rugby life, and I felt proud at the time that it was him doing it, dragging me to the ground and shoving my head in the dirt.

The pitch is a place I feel comfortable on. Inwardly I'm thinking, 'This is what I know, this is my livelihood, I feel confident in my knowledge of this game.' It's about knowing your job and doing it. You could compare it to going into an exam knowing you're fully prepared. You don't want to be worrying that you haven't covered the last chapter or something. If you're not fully prepared, fear can crop up in pressure situations. You can forget a call for a split-second, you can be unsure of what move to call in a certain part of the pitch.

> **WHEN I WAS A BOY PEOPLE WOULD SAY I WAS TOO SMALL TO PLAY RUGBY. I'D GET LOOKS FROM THE OPPOSITION, FELLAS SAYING, 'WHAT'S THIS GUY DOING HERE? IS HE FOR REAL?'**

When I'm out there it's like I'm in a comfort zone, but not in a bad way, not in a complacent way. I feel there's an onus on me to speak and I know I can do that without letting myself down. Maybe before I might have worried if guys respected me enough to say it to them. But now I know I can stand up in front of them and say, 'Look, we've got to make sure this is done. If there's an opportunity for us to run it here we need six guys showing as an option, if it's on.' Simple things, but important things. Just saying that lifts the worry off my own shoulders. I know I'm not going be sitting there after the final whistle thinking, 'Shit, if only I'd gone to him and made sure he knew.'

Outside of rugby, I prefer to stand off more, to be an onlooker. I feel comfortable talking to people one on one, but I tend to be a bit shy in public situations because I don't want to risk making a fool of myself if things come up that I'm not too sure about. It's like being in a lecture in college when you don't know what's going on around you and you're kind of shy and reserved.

Nobody likes to hear negative things said about them. Early in my career it put doubts in my mind and tested my mentality, my character as a rugby player. Being continuously put down in the press after matches, it did affect me. I'd be lying if I said otherwise. I would think, 'Jesus, I'm representing my country, and guys who've been watching rugby and writing about it for years are saying these things about me.' It creeps into your mind and you start questioning yourself. Am I fit for this international game? But as I became more experienced I got confidence from speaking to coaches and people I respected, from my friends and my family and my team-mates. I got confidence from being selected on teams, getting cap after cap, from more and more people saying to me, 'What are these people writing?'

When you look back on what we have achieved as a team over the years, that other stuff is irrelevant. I'm just glad that I've been a part of it. The support I've had from a lot of people in Munster has been very special and very important to me. It's an incredible feeling to know that they respect me.

CHAPTER 6
THE MIRACLE AND THE BIG STING

❝ THERE WAS JUST PURE JOY, PURE HAPPINESS EVERYWHERE. ❞

Jim Williams, by now a hero among the Munster faithful, was named team captain after Mick Galwey handed over the armband. The new coach was another Australian, hired from Leinster. Alan Gaffney had been assistant to Matt Williams, charged with making an already outstanding backline even better. It was an enjoyable job, but it wasn't stretching Gaffney. He felt he had more to give. When Leinster dragged their heels about renewing his contract he started thinking about what the future held. Then Munster made an approach, and before he knew it Gaffney was headed south, excited but full of trepidation.

He wondered how the players would come back from losing a second European Cup final in three seasons. He questioned whether he would be good enough to lead such a team from the front, but he knew he had to be true to the motto he has lived his life by – 'never die wondering'.

When he arrived, Gaffney put a question to Galwey. What was it, he wanted to know, that made Munster special? The big Kerryman did not hesitate.

'It's the X-factor.'

'The X-factor? What's that?'

'I haven't a clue.'

If it was all change at the top, there was something different, too, about the way Munster's European odyssey resumed a few months later, in October 2002. For the first time in five years they were on the road for the first match. Their destination was Kingsholm, fortress of the unbeaten English Premiership leaders Gloucester, where Sale, Bristol and Saracens had all shipped forty points plus. Never had they been asked a bigger question in the opening match of the tournament, and this time there was no answer: in winning 35–16 Gloucester scored four tries and earned a bonus point. In truth, their victory could have been even more emphatic.

Munster picked up the pieces and put three wins together, but when they went to Perpignan on the second Saturday in January they were battered into submission, losing 23–8. The task ahead of them at Thomond Park a week later, for the visit of Gloucester, was so monumental that few were aware of the full extent of it. The facts, though, were these: Munster needed to outscore Gloucester by four tries and win the match by a minimum of twenty-seven points. By now Gloucester were eight points clear at the top of the Premiership, and the lead did not flatter them. They brought an army of supporters with them to Limerick, 2,000 strong. They had the momentum of a juggernaut. Munster had just put up their worst performance of the season, for which the match reports read like obituaries.

MARK SOUSTER, *THE TIMES*: Is this the end of an era? One suspects so. All teams have a natural life span and the evidence after this heavy defeat must be that Munster are reaching the end of theirs.

BRENDAN GALLAGHER, *DAILY TELEGRAPH*: Almost anything is possible at Thomond Park, where Munster boast a 100 per cent record over eight seasons in the Heineken Cup, but nobody seriously expects Gloucester to cave in so spectacularly … Munster are creaking up front and vulnerable at home like never before. Gloucester, worthy leaders of the Premiership, have nothing to fear and possess the firepower to take Munster's proud record.

COLM KEYES, *IRISH MIRROR*: Munster won't survive in the competition beyond today – that much we can be fairly certain of. The notion of them scoring four tries more than Gloucester is scarcely believable. Munster don't do their business that way, as a glance back at some of their most momentous afternoons in Thomond would verify. Their favoured route to victory is the tight, thundering war of attrition. Munster have not bothered themselves with calculators and permutations this week either, almost as if they sense that a place beyond the pool is gone for this year and that retaining the mystique of Thomond is a priority. Deep down they know this is about pride.

JOHN KELLY: To be fair, you couldn't really criticize any journalist for writing us off after the Perpignan match. In a nice way, we were being written off by our own supporters. They were coming up to us saying, 'Thanks for everything, it's been great.' For most people out there, it felt like the end. It was depressing.

ANTHONY FOLEY: They were saying, 'Thanks for the year – and let's just finish it off now by beating Gloucester.' All week Alan [Gaffney] drummed it into us to just concentrate on the process of the game, not to get too carried away with the scoreline. The plan was to win – and see where that got us. Did we think it was possible to go through? Of course. I did an interview for BBC, and they asked me which was more important – qualifying for the quarter-final or maintaining our home record in Thomond Park? I remember thinking to myself, 'Lose? We don't lose in Thomond Park. That is just not going to happen.' But to suggest we were going to hammer the Premiership leaders would have been a very arrogant statement, so I said 'maintaining our record'.

FRANKIE SHEAHAN: At the start of the week our heads were hanging. We had a scrummaging session in training, and the first few scrums were poor. I said, 'Look, lads, we'd better sort this. We might be going out, but we can't let these fellas beat us in Thomond Park.' Axel said the same, and that was the start of the fightback.

> **TO BE FAIR, YOU COULDN'T REALLY CRITICIZE ANY JOURNALIST FOR WRITING US OFF AFTER THE PERPIGNAN MATCH. IN A NICE WAY, WE WERE BEING WRITTEN OFF BY OUR OWN SUPPORTERS. THEY WERE COMING UP TO US SAYING, 'THANKS FOR EVERYTHING, IT'S BEEN GREAT.'**

> **AT THE START OF THE WEEK OUR HEADS WERE HANGING. WE HAD A SCRUMMAGING SESSION IN TRAINING, AND THE FIRST FEW SCRUMS WERE POOR. I SAID, 'LOOK, LADS, WE'D BETTER SORT THIS.'**

My mother cooked a dinner for me that Wednesday night, and my dad was in the TV room with pen and paper, working out what we needed to do. He was saying, 'Take a look at this – what ye need is …'

I said, 'Look, sorry, but I'm not interested. We just need to win. We can't lose our unbeaten record.' He wouldn't let it go, though. He was starting to annoy me. He went on about it so much that two numbers stuck in my head.

Four tries. Twenty-seven points.

ALAN QUINLAN: People were saying prayers for us that week – we needed a miracle. My mother, Mary Quinlan, is a holy person. Anywhere there's been a miracle, she's been there – Fatima, Lourdes, Medjugorje, everywhere. She has stacks of holy water from all over the world. Anyone will tell you that when you come into our house in Tipperary you're always going to get a good lash of holy water when you're leaving. John Hayes is always getting it. So is Rog. She has it in bottles and she's always giving me some to put in my bag before a match. She gets bottles to Pat Geraghty, and he goes around blessing the lads and throwing holy water on them. If ever there was a day when we needed it, that was the day.

The drab concrete stand at Thomond Park was built in the early eighties and will be razed in 2007, to make way for a replacement fit for the modern age, but on that January day it was rocking. For a player sitting in a dressing room underneath it is impossible not to hear the noise sweeping in from the terraces on days like this. Once upon a time, when the stand was made of timber, people stamped hard on the floorboards directly overhead, and sometimes it felt like hundreds of feet were about to come crashing though the ceiling. The noise you hear from the sanctuary of the visiting dressing room is more distant and less threatening now. It is only when you run down the narrow path leading to the pitch that it seems to rise up and hit you full in the face. Just in case you haven't got the message, some young Munster pup will lean over the barrier running the length of the pathway and scream at you. Welcome to Thomond Park.

Two minutes before kick-off, up in the stand, a legend of the Shannon club called Frankie O'Flynn picked up a microphone and started singing. By the time the Gloucester out-half Ludovic Mercier launched the ball deep into the Munster twenty-two, he was still on his feet, only halfway through 'Stand Up and Fight', a lone voice amplified above the cauldron.

Everyone knew that Henry Paul, the Gloucester full-back, was going to be provided with a little test of his nerve at the first opportunity. Ronan O'Gara, like a legion of Munster kickers before him, would launch a garryowen into the heavens. It was only a matter of time. It was going to happen because it always happened.

O'Gara waited six minutes before firing the ball down the full-back's throat. It spun off his right boot as he struck it, which only made things worse for Paul. The ball was in the air for 4.6 seconds. It swerved high over Paul's head at its apogee, so that he was forced to turn on his heels and run deeper into his own half in pursuit. In the crescendo of noise as the ball began its descent, Paul's feet moved this way and that as he tried desperately to position himself under it. A huge roar went up when it bounced high over his head and Paul stole a half-glance to his left, where the first Munster player in pursuit was seven strides away. He wrapped his scarlet gloves around the ball a split-second before Mike Mullins crashed into him and managed to stay on his feet, but the reprieve was temporary. Jason Holland, the second Munster centre, arrived next, and as more red shirts poured forward Henry Paul was spreadeagled across the turf on all fours, like a man with no balance on a skating rink. For him, and for Gloucester, things would go downhill from there.

Seventeen minutes in, John Kelly put the first try on the board. Deep in first-half stoppage time, Mossy Lawlor made it two. Ahead 16–6 at the break, Munster knew for sure now that it was on, and the old crowd shook with excitement at what might be ahead. With O'Gara working the corners, the third try came on the hour, brilliantly

John Kelly dives for a first-half try; later he would score the crucial fourth try . . .

scored by the mighty Mick O'Driscoll. 'The dander was up then,' Foley would reflect. O'Gara kicked the extras and Munster were within one converted try of their miracle.

Then, a reprieve that might have come from above. With eight minutes on the clock, Quinlan was penalized directly in front of his own posts, 22 metres out. Gloucester had a kick that would have put them through, a penalty Mercier would have slotted with his eyes closed. But Mercier wasn't thinking straight, or maybe he hadn't bothered to do the maths. He tapped and ran, into the abyss. It seemed fated after that. In the final seconds of normal time, with their supporters screaming for the fourth try, Munster surged ever closer to the Gloucester line. Jeremy Staunton barrelled ahead and was nailed. Red shirts piled into the ruck.

JOHN KELLY: I was screaming and screaming for it to come out. It seemed to take an age. We had men over, but slowly they were moving across to cover us. Anthony Foley was outside me. We both knew that fast ball meant a try – and the ball was fast. Peter did a brilliant job to dig it out. I went over but wasn't sure if that was good enough. Did we need the conversion or not? I didn't know. All I knew was that we were close, and that the fans were going wild. They said they were 2,000 fans from Gloucester, but I didn't hear them. All I heard was cries of 'Munster', all day long.

ANTHONY FOLEY: Fellows were saying four tries were enough, but Frankie Sheahan was adamant that we needed to win by twenty-seven points. Nobody told Rog, because he thought the job was done when he was taking the conversion. In fairness to the lad, if you were to put your money on anybody to kick it for you it would be him.

. . . which Ronan O'Gara duly converted

RONAN O'GARA: I had to kick it anyway, for my own standards. Whether I knew or not wasn't that relevant, in my opinion. It wouldn't have made a difference to me.

DONNCHA O'CALLAGHAN: When Rog's kick went over a supporter ran over to me shouting, 'We've done it! We've qualified!' I started to jump around like a little schoolgirl. I grabbed a hold of Jim Williams, I was delirious. I still watch the end of that match and cringe – but there was just pure joy, pure happiness everywhere. And there I am in the middle of it, jumping around like an idiot.

STEPHEN JONES, *THE SUNDAY TIMES*: It was one of those occasions where you have sit down in a quiet place afterwards, to try to work out whether you actually dreamed it.

Flushed with victory and barely able to contain himself, Alan Gaffney described it as 'the greatest, most magnificent result I have ever been involved in. The Munster spirit? I guess I understood maybe half of what that phrase means before today. Now, I understand the whole of it. It is an awesome thing, staggering.'

Munster were rewarded with a brutally tough quarter-final draw, away to Leicester, who were seeking their third Heineken Cup in a row. In almost six years they had been defeated at Welford Road only twice. The build-up was dominated by media talk of revenge for Neil Back's sleight of hand, but Munster had moved on. For them, the day wasn't about Back, it was about proving they were a good team.

ALAN QUINLAN: We were on fire in the dressing room. We were like wild animals trying to get out on the field. A lot of it, I think, was the fear factor – playing against such a great Leicester team. We realized we had an opportunity to make it into one of the great days.

DONNCHA O'CALLAGHAN: It was a day when everyone in the pack was trying to outdo each other. When that happens, it's huge. When I see Paulie carry a ball, I want to do the same and make more ground. It's nearly competitive. And he's the most competitive man around.

Playing against Martin Johnson was a big thing for me. I remember at a crucial

 Opposite: **On the Thomond Park balcony afterwards, it was pandemonium**

Leicester's talisman was the England captain, Martin Johnson (with ball)

stage in the game I slipped off my boot because we needed time. We were ahead, but under pressure. He saw it and he shouted at me …

'Get up there! Jesus!'

He was telling the referee that I'd clearly kicked off my boot, and I kept thinking, 'I have so much respect for this man to have a go back here.' He was looking at me, and I nearly even said it, like. I almost said, 'I've too much respect to talk shit to you.' For me he's been a hero since I was a teenager. I would have hated it if I'd said something that embarrassed me.

One day when I was younger I had to go up to Liam Toland after a game and apologize to the man because of what I'd said. He's good friends with my brother Ultan, and I knew I'd said bad things. I knew Martin Johnson was expecting me to come out with something. There was this look on his face. 'Why isn't this fella opening his mouth?' But I just kept my head down, threw on my boot and ran back.

Mike Mullins breaks through the Leicester defence, flanked by Rob Henderson

A while after that we kicked into them, and I ended up landing on my head because I was trying to get to the ball so much. I was left stranded in an awful position, and it could have been dangerous if anyone had come across or fallen on me. I didn't know it at the time, but on the video you can see him [Johnson] looking over at me and then pushing me back on to my side, helping me out of the dangerous position I was in.

ROB HENDERSON: I'd been to Welford Road numerous times with London Irish and Wasps and never won. I'd seen some great tries, sometimes seven in a game, nearly all to them. It was always going to be a tough, tough match. I was at fault for Geordan Murphy's try, which put them ahead by a point. I ran out of the line to smash him, and Twinkletoes took one step back, one to the right and off he went and scored in the corner. I wasn't happy with myself but I tried to keep the head. After the kick-off,

there was a scrum just left of the posts and Austin [Healey] and Leon Lloyd were doing a switch. Two seconds before I had turned around to Rog and said, 'If they do a switch, I'm smashing him.' I ran up, clipped Austin and Lloydie at the same time and the two of them fell on the floor. Austin was in a bit of trouble. Knock-on, five phases later Rog scores. I've made up for the missed tackle – now let's get on with the match.

MARCUS HORAN: We knew we'd won when Strings scored our second try. You can win a lot of games and not enjoy playing in them. You can probably lose games that you do enjoy playing. That was one game that we won and loved every minute. We'd gone into the Tigers' den and beaten them. Our supporters even intimidated their players that day, they were just amazing. Going back out to the crowd afterwards, the emotion of that, is one of best memories I have in rugby.

It was my first season as a regular in the team and it was a big boost for me,

Donncha O'Callaghan celebrates the revenge victory over Leicester

WE'D GONE INTO THE TIGERS' DEN AND BEATEN THEM. OUR SUPPORTERS EVEN INTIMIDATED THEIR PLAYERS THAT DAY, THEY WERE JUST AMAZING.

personally. I'd been fighting for my place for a couple of years, up against Peter Clohessy. People had been saying, 'Hang in there, he's going to retire,' but I wanted to be there on merit. I didn't want anyone to think I was just waiting for my turn. I was fighting hard all the way.

DONNCHA O'CALLAGHAN: I always looked up to people like Mick Galwey, but for me Martin Johnson was out on his own. Maybe because I didn't know him – he was just this giant of world rugby. One of the reasons I wanted to play well in that game so much was because I wanted him to think I was a good player. It was an incredible thing for him to say 'Well done' to me at the end.

ROB HENDERSON: After everything that had happened, we were starting to think it was going to be our year. The final was going to be at Lansdowne Road. But we got the short straw again in the semi-final – Toulouse away.

The day before, we trained at this ground near by and we were worried about them spying on us. Brian Hickey, our lineout coach, should be in intelligence or something. He was scanning the place, looking for people who might have had a camera. We were getting a great kick out of it.

'Brian, there's someone over there – behind the bush.'

'Brian, that fella with the screwdriver fixing a light? He could have a camera on him.'

'Check that dog's collar – there could be something on it.'

And away he would go, towel over one shoulder, ball under one arm, shuffling off.

Fair play to the Munster supporters, all 12,000 of them, they didn't let us down. The big air-raid sirens were firing off at one end, but our fans were just as noisy. What do I remember? Just that it was a very tough match against a very good side. Trevor Brennan was storming around the place. We tried to play running rugby but we didn't have the wherewithal to break them down. They scored one try, we scored none. Another one-point loss – not quite good enough. Again. But you have to keep going. And that is the bloodline of this team. If you get knocked back, there's someone behind you who will stand up and lift you and carry you on to the next goal. For any other team it would have been fatal to be beaten so many times by less than seven points in semi-finals and finals. They wouldn't have been able to pick themselves up, time and again.

ANTHONY FOLEY: The one thing we took out of the Toulouse game was the size of their squad – they had a who's who of French rugby on their bench. After that, we said that if we were ever going to win this competition we'd need internationals on our bench too.

Paul O'Connell fends off a Toulouse tackle

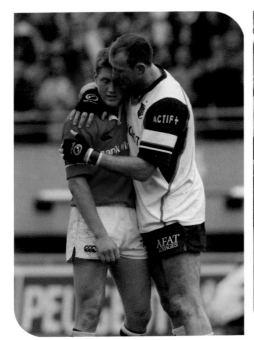

Afterwards: Toulouse's Irishman Trevor Brennan consoles Ronan O'Gara (left), and, after swapping shirts, Alan Gaffney (right)

Gaffney had already begun the job of adding depth to his squad, especially in the backline. Five weeks before the defeat of Leicester, he had confirmed his interest in Chris Latham, the Australia full-back. Latham signed a letter of intent to join Munster and then pulled out, to Gaffney's anger. But then another celebrated Antipodean full-back came on the market, and Munster made their move.

Christian Cullen was the most prolific try-scorer in All Black history. Still only twenty-seven, he had been controversially omitted from New Zealand's World Cup squad that autumn. His manager flew over to check the lie of the land and liked what he saw. Cullen signed for three years and flew into Cork airport in November. A few days later he was given the demoralizing news that a shoulder injury sustained in his final match for Wellington needed surgery. He would miss the entire pool stage of the 2003–2004 Heineken Cup.

He was not the only new signing, however. Into the side at full-back came Shaun Payne, a 31-year-old South African with a grandmother from Sligo.

SHAUN PAYNE: I played ninety-odd games for Natal Sharks. My final year there was 1999, when the whole side was breaking up. Gary Teichmann, Andre Joubert, Henry Honiball – they were all leaving. Out of the blue I got an offer to come and play for

Swansea. You could earn a lot more in Europe back then. I had four seasons there, and then the club went into administration. I wasn't very happy about that, I thought it was a cop-out. Just when that was happening, Alan phoned me. He said, 'How would you feel about joining Munster?' I said, 'Thank you very much – I'd love to join Munster.'

In my first year we came top in a pool with Gloucester, Bourgoin and Treviso. I'd heard all abut the win against Gloucester the previous season, and we put four tries on them again at Thomond Park. Christian was at full-back for the quarter-final against Stade Français, and I was picked on the wing. That was a home match, and it wasn't easy, but we managed to get through it. Into the semi-final, then, against Wasps at Lansdowne Road. I'll never forget seeing all the Munster supporters on the way to the ground. It was just incredible.

CHRISTIAN CULLEN: Those first months were tough, coming here injured and not knowing anybody. But I had a good spell when I came back from the shoulder injury, and the bus journey to the ground for the Wasps match was a great feeling for me. There was Munster red everywhere.

ROBERT KITSON, *GUARDIAN*: It is quite possible that Munster versus Wasps in front of a record semi-final audience of 48,000 in Dublin will be the most seismic occasion in the Heineken Cup's illustrious history. To paraphrase Wasps' director of rugby, Warren Gatland, it is as if the red Munster jersey has mythical properties, such is the Asterix-style transformation among those who pull it on. Yet Wasps are playing with a murderous intensity, and no one who witnessed their demolition of Gloucester in the quarter-final was left in any doubt they will confront the challenge without blinking.

ROB HENDERSON: Will Green said Wasps were doing lineouts in the hotel car park, and the crowd all around them were Munster supporters, just hurling abuse. He knew then it was going to be hostile. They all came out looking like rugby league players. Tight jerseys and what have you.

SHAUN PAYNE: We lost Rog early on, but Jason Holland came on and was playing well. They had scored a couple of tries in the first half, but then Axel scored, and we were in front. About four or five minutes later, Jimmy scored, and the place erupted. I remember hearing the noise and thinking, 'I will never hear anything like that again.' I thought we had the match sewn up.

ANTHONY FOLEY: Just stop the video with ten minutes to go and leave it at that – go away happy. From being ten points up, suddenly it started to fall apart. We didn't have the patience and the control that we needed, that we'd have these days. It was disappointing because we had worked so hard to get into position after conceding a couple of soft tries in the first half. But you can't finish out a game with thirteen players and hope to win it against the best side in England.

PAUL O'CONNELL: Looking back on that game – and on other big games we lost – my feeling is that we were going out giving everything, but were we playing to win? There's a difference there. You've got to go out there and try to dominate a match. Did we have the mentality of champions? No, we weren't there yet.

Anthony Foley touches down in the semi-final against Wasps at Lansdowne Road, April 2004: 'Just stop the video with ten minutes to go and leave it at that – go away happy'

Ronan O'Gara kicks for goal, in front of a hoarding announcing the final that Munster would not reach

DONNCHA O'CALLAGHAN: I got sent to the sin-bin for playing the ball on the ground. I've watched that game and I've got no problem saying it was incredibly harsh. We'd only given away a few penalties; they had sixteen against them. Sitting there for those ten minutes, watching the lads battle, was a desperate feeling.

ROB HENDERSON: Late in the game, after Donncha had been binned, we were under all sorts of pressure, and a ruck was being formed. I was ambling back as best I could at that stage, because everyone was exhausted. We'd put in a lot of effort. I thought I'd got onside. The ball came out, Alex King picked it up, and I tackled him. Offside. Yellow card. That's it, that's you done for the day. We were down to thirteen for the last few minutes. I was just devastated. I wanted a hole to open up and swallow me. To watch that from the bench, with the lads working so hard, and then to see Trevor Leota score a try that should never have been given was so hard to take.

DONNCHA O'CALLAGHAN: I sat in the dressing room afterwards and I've never felt guilt like it in my life. I looked around and I caught eyes with John Hayes. He just gave me a nod, as if to say, 'Are you all right?' I remember thinking, 'How can you be nice to me? I've let you down.' I just felt so guilty. After that game I got on to [the former referee] Dave McHugh. I told him, 'Dave, I need to know more about referees and the way they think.' I know it was a harsh decision, but for the ten minutes I wasn't on the pitch I let those guys down and I still feel that way.

DENIS LEAMY: I was injured that season, so I went to the game with my girlfriend, Antoinette. I've been to Ireland games and come out after losing, and people wouldn't be that bothered. That day, it was like someone had died. People were so quiet – they couldn't talk, they were so upset.

ALAN QUINLAN: We learned from that. It was a very, very important game for us. If you want to be the best in Europe you've got to keep raising the bar and looking for things to get better at. We realized we needed to be fitter and stronger. Wasps were ten points down with ten minutes to go but they didn't panic, and their fitness pulled them through. We got feedback from the Wasps players about their training regime, the amount of fitness people they had, the amount of weights they did, their nutritionists and dieticians. We had fantastically dedicated people in our back-room staff, but we just didn't have that level of attention to detail and we had to find it. Credit to the management – they changed a lot of things and gave us more support. At that level, it's as good as Test match rugby – it's probably more intense because there's more passion there with the supporters.

ANTHONY FOLEY: Everything was put in place for us. Garrett [Fitzgerald, chief executive] and Holl [Jerry Holland, team manager] are reasonable people. Once everybody can benefit from it, there are no qualms. They'll bend over backwards to make sure we have everything we require.

For the first time in six seasons, Munster failed to make the semi-finals the following year. Once again they headed their pool – ahead of Harlequins, Castres and Neath-Swansea Ospreys – but they ended up one bonus point short for a home quarter-final. Faced with a powerfully equipped Biarritz in the cauldron of Estadio Anoeta in San Sebastian, they conceded sixteen unanswered points in the first half. They fought their way back into it, but there was too much ground to make up. It ended Biarritz 19, Munster 10.

For Alan Gaffney, it was the end of the line. After three years as coach, he had accepted an offer to return home and join the Australia coaching staff. On his leaving day six weeks later there was a trophy to celebrate, but nobody pretended that beating Llanelli Scarlets in the Celtic Cup final was anything other than a nice way for a nice man to go out. As the players did a lap of honour, Shaun Payne walked over to Anthony Foley. 'This doesn't feel right,' he said. 'We're parading with the wrong trophy.'

By then, the new Munster coach had already been appointed. On the day of the semi-final in San Sebastian, a newspaper report had linked Declan Kidney to his old job. Kidney, after two years as assistant to Eddie O'Sullivan with Ireland, had been Leinster's coach for just over ten months. Twenty-four hours before Munster's European exit, Leinster had been comprehensively beaten by Leicester at a packed Lansdowne Road. Once it became known that Kidney had applied for the Munster job, his departure from Leinster was swift. It was also rancorous. In the newspapers, Kidney was charged with leaving Leinster in the lurch.

DECLAN KIDNEY: People wrote what they wrote. They wrote what they thought was right, I suppose. They didn't ask me to explain it. It wasn't a decision that I made lightly – there was a huge cost in doing it. I enjoyed my year in Leinster and I worked with some brilliant people. I don't think I did too badly. We had six great Heineken Cup days and one bad one. There was only one reason for moving and that was being closer to home. If I hadn't done it and something had happened at home while I'd been away I could never have forgiven myself.

I didn't pick the time, I didn't do any of that. It was a job that was advertised. I don't know of anybody in any work situation who doesn't want to work closer to home. I'd like to think I'm no different to any other person. Every so often in life you just have to make decisions, and this was something I just had to do.

As things turned out, I was lucky enough to be back living in Cork when my mother was well. Then she got sick at the end of November, and I was able to stay in the hospital with her. I couldn't have done that had I been with Leinster. She died just after Christmas. I don't know, maybe the man above said, 'You need to get home.'

Of course I had doubts. I didn't like letting people down. It wouldn't have been justifiable if I hadn't made the decision for the reasons that I did. It wasn't easy for anybody. But if something doesn't kill you, it will make you stronger.

The Munster job I came back to and the one I left were two totally different things. It was a much bigger organization, with fifty people depending on it for their living. But at the heart of it all was the same goal as before: winning the Heineken Cup. There were the same core values and basic standards and there was the same honesty among the players. Their ambition to do well is so great that if it doesn't happen they are going to be microscopically self-critical. They are a very self-critical bunch, and that's good, most of the time. But not when you are so self-critical that it becomes a burden and it holds you back.

CHAPTER 7
PAUL O'CONNELL'S STORY

❝ OUR PEOPLE ONLY ACCEPT EXCELLENCE. ❞

If you're good enough you can take criticism – you can take the most harsh, most vicious criticism from the people you're working with, the guys who just want to be better. I really believe that. It's the only way I improved at the start of my career. If you're good enough to play for Munster, you're good enough to take it because in this game you've got to be mentally strong. In the end, on the biggest days, the strongest team is the one left standing.

With Munster, the criticism comes from the players. In the beginning I didn't like it. I thought, 'This will break people.' Deccie wouldn't be big into it either. But we're hard on ourselves because we know we need to keep improving. Muhammad Ali said, 'If I were a garbage man, I'd be the world's greatest garbage man.' The day you stop striving to be better is the day you start getting worse. I consider myself miles off my potential as a player, and a lot of the other guys in the Munster squad feel the same way. I could be faster, I could be fitter, I could be more skilful. Some things I keep to myself, but I know I need to work massively on them. That's the beauty of rugby. You've got to be powerful, you've to be fast and agile, you've got to have the skills, you've got to know the lineout calls and so many other things. It's the decathlon of team sport.

There's a lot of pressure in defending our unbeaten record at Thomond Park. If you're confident in your ability, pressure makes you play better, not worse. Our supporters expect us to win, and there is something un-Irish about that, a serious shift in mentality.

Look at New Zealand – if they don't win they get murdered. It doesn't matter that they've given it 100 per cent – they still get murdered. Americans go to the Olympics and they expect to win all the gold medals. In Munster our supporters expect success, and I love that, it's one of the best things about this whole movement. One of the great beauties and the great tragedies of Irish sport is that the 'give it a lash' attitude is good enough. We've moved on from that in Munster. Our people only accept excellence. We don't want a pat on the back if we go down fighting.

In my family we were spoiled growing up, in the sense that any sport we wanted to do we were given the option. Me and my brothers, Justin and Marcus, we dabbled in everything. We had no interest in Super Nintendo computer games or anything like that. They wouldn't have been bought for us anyway. We had a huge back garden out in the country, and it was all about sport for us.

I was the youngest, and when you've got a brother who's a year and nine months older it's a massive thing for you to keep up with him. If you're always being beaten it builds a bit of bitterness and a bit of competitiveness in you. Once you leave the pitch those things can be bad, but as a professional player they're the best qualities you can have. People in Limerick have a chip on their shoulder, and I've got that. It's inbred. Limerick is looked down on in every way except for rugby. We've grown up with it, and for a lot of us it's our strongest weapon. Ask anyone who has gone to a match with my dad: he's an absolute gentleman, until it kicks off. Then the abuse comes out of him. I get agitated when I'm watching matches too. I'd be very one-eyed when I'm on the sideline.

Whatever sport I've played, I've tended to get into it in a big way. You learn different things from different coaches. So many people in Limerick have had an influence on me I wouldn't know where to start, but they know who they are, and I'm grateful to every one of them. When you spend time with these people, just hanging around them, you become a bit streetwise.

I started playing rugby when I was six or seven – my dad brought me up to his club, Young Munster. Then I got into swimming. I used to train for two hours before going to school, in the evening and at weekends. Then I took up golf and I worked hard at that, got my handicap down to four and hit a wall. Couldn't get any lower.

I went back to the rugby at sixteen and played for my school, Ardscoil Rís. I got a few breaks and I was on my way. Even though I'd come to it a bit late, I had a good work ethic and I think that's what Munster took a chance on.

ONE OF THE GREAT BEAUTIES AND THE GREAT TRAGEDIES OF IRISH SPORT IS THAT THE 'GIVE IT A LASH' ATTITUDE IS GOOD ENOUGH. WE'VE MOVED ON FROM THAT IN MUNSTER. OUR PEOPLE ONLY ACCEPT EXCELLENCE. WE DON'T WANT A PAT ON THE BACK IF WE GO DOWN FIGHTING.

That's the big thing down here – people enjoy working hard, and the plaudits and the big wins only come with hard work. Some people get lucky in sport – a lot of lesser players than Roy Keane have won the European Cup – but generally speaking you get out of it what you put into it.

Rugby is non-stop confrontation, and you've got to be physically and mentally up for it. You see guys at the end of their careers, just doing it for the money and playing like a bucket of shite, and you think, 'I saw that guy five years ago, and he was just incredible.' To be successful you've to believe in what you're playing for 100 per cent. I know if I lost that I'd be a very average player.

I think we're fortunate in that we don't have any absolute superstars, people who carve it up and score three tries. A guy like Rog is obviously a fabulous player – he's been delivering at the top level for eight years – but you don't see him scoring tries from 100 yards out. For us to succeed, everyone has to work their socks off and everyone has to get on with each other. That's what we have in Munster. That's the beauty of the whole thing – after a few months in there you feel like you've been there for ever.

CHAPTER 8
NEW BLOOD, NEW FOCUS

❝ PUT THAT INTO THE BITTERNESS BANK. ❞

FEDERICO PUCCIARIELLO: I come from Rosario in Argentina, but for a long time I have played rugby in Europe. Before he left, Alan Gaffney contacted me and asked me to join Munster. It was for me a new challenge. Completely different. So I take the challenge.

Some people can play just one position and they are the best in the country. I can play in all the three positions of the front row. That is my strongest quality. In France, I played one game in the three positions. It is my way.

The front row at Munster is the Irish front row, but it was quite the same case when I went to England and Gloucester. They had Vickery and Woodman. So I like that kind of challenge.

You have two sides to rugby. One is mental. And I think if your head is good you can play well. And when I arrive in Ireland – and I say Ireland, not just Munster – there was a huge welcome. And that was a huge surprise because I didn't know that before. That helped me a lot.

TREVOR HALSTEAD: It was a touchy time for me back at the Sharks. I wasn't getting on with the coach and I was just unhappy. I had given the Sharks a lot of years. I'm a Sharks boy, I've been brought up on that and it's all I wanted, but I got snubbed at the end. My agent went in to negotiate a new contract, and their offer was an absolute joke, half of what I was on before. Then I heard Munster were interested in me. It was like a destiny thing. I knew they were always competitive in the Heineken Cup, and that's all I needed to know. I wanted a new experience, away from South Africa.

I signed on the Monday, and on the Wednesday the Sharks fired Kevin Putt, the coach. That same day the new coaching staff got hold of me and said, 'Please, we want

Opposite: Enter stage right: Federico Pucciariello was one of several Munster newcomers in 2005–2006 who would contribute to the team's European triumph

MUNSTER: OUR ROAD TO GLORY 123

you to stay. You're starting our next game.' I said, 'I've gotta tell you guys – I've signed with Munster.' They were trying to get me out of it, but I'm very glad I made the move.

ANTHONY FOLEY: We like people who want to prove a point, people with a bit of bitterness in them. They buy into what we're about. It goes back to our club rugby days. The All Ireland League has been dominated by Munster teams because they wouldn't back down.

Coming into the new season, there were issues that we needed to rectify – dealing with the hype around big games. We were planning on being in the final and we had to make sure we were going to be mentally right if we got there. Declan was doing everything in his power to make sure that every player had everything he needed to perform. He brought Declan Aherne in to help us on the mental side of things. We knew we would have to perform for eighty minutes if we were ever going to win it. We had some new blood in the squad and other guys pushing hard to get in. Good competition for places, a real buzz in the camp. We had learned from our defeats and we'll never stop learning from them, but there comes a point you either take the lessons fully on board or you get out of the class. There comes a time when you have to just go and win this thing.

RONAN O'GARA: Pre-season was horrible, the hardest we've ever known it. Pure mental torture, but there's no substitute for that kind of hard work. It's challenging mentally and it improves you both physically and aerobically.

JERRY FLANNERY: It's very hard to get a run in this side. It does take an injury. I did a good pre-season, played against Northampton and Leicester, and Declan said he was giving me my start in the first Celtic League match. He said Frankie [Sheahan] would start the next match and after that he'd go on performances. So we played the Borders at Thomond Park and we barely beat them, 11–10 or something. It was a fairly sticky performance, and the media were saying, 'Oh, Munster don't look great this year – sloppy performance against Borders, the worst side in the Celtic League.'

I sat out the next match, and Munster destroyed the Ospreys, absolutely hammered them. They had won the Celtic League the year before, but I was looking at them

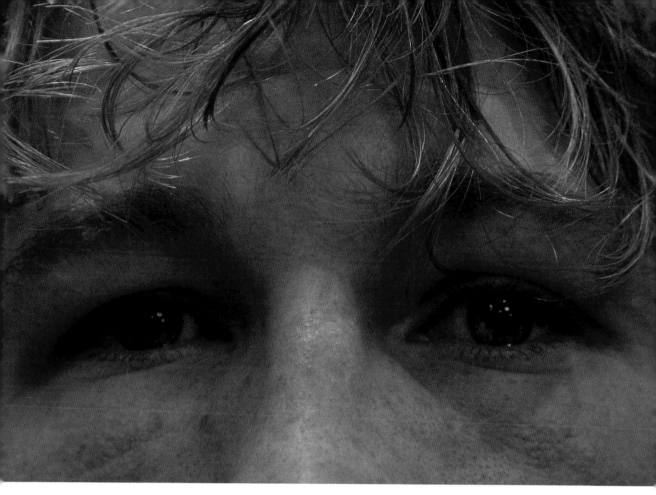

Jerry Flannery

thinking, 'They are rubbish!' They didn't play at all. Next thing all the papers were going, 'Munster! What a performance – thrashed the champions!'

And I was like, 'For fuck's sake. Back to square one again here.'

The following week I was sitting on the bench against Glasgow, and Declan said, 'You guys are in the form of your lives, you're in the prime of your careers.' I just sat there thinking, 'If I'm in the prime of my career then I'm sitting here wasting it. I'm twenty-seven years old and when I look back on my career, I'll have been sat on the bench for most of it.'

In the European Cup we were in a pool with Sale, Castres and Newport-Gwent Dragons. The first match was away to Sale, and I knew I wouldn't be starting. Every time you picked up the paper that week there was an article about how good Sale were. Top of the Premiership. The pressure was on because if you lose your first match you're seriously up against it.

Roy Keane, who spent two hours talking with the team the night before the Sale match, watches intently from the stand

PAT GERAGHTY: The night before the Sale game we had arranged for Roy Keane to visit our hotel. At first the players were just told that we had a surprise visitor, but when he didn't show at the appointed time, their attitude was, 'Screw him, whoever he was.' They started doing different things – Federico was playing Monopoly. Next thing Keano turned up – he'd been taken to the wrong hotel – and he had the lads absolutely enthralled. Just as he was finishing, Puccy went back to his game. We were thanking Roy outside, just saying our goodbyes, and he says, 'Ah, no problem, lads, delighted to do it, hope I was OK with 'em. I kinda knew it time to wind it up when I saw yer man starting to play the Monopoly.'

Puccy hadn't a clue who Roy Keane was. The next day we were in Manchester and he saw a big poster of him. He goes, 'Ah, this is the guy who is in the hotel last night. Roy Keane – he plays football, yes?'

ANTHONY FOLEY: Roy Keane had the room for two hours. Everybody was just enthralled with what he said. The ambition he has shown in his career is an example to all of us.

He always wanted extra things to improve his team's performance, and we're entitled to do the exact same thing, to demand more out of the organization.

The next day we couldn't get over how negative Sale were – how they just kept kicking the ball away and turning us the whole time. We were waiting for them to cut loose and play a bit of rugby so that we could try and turn them over. It was very frustrating.

ALAN QUINLAN: I was running past Mark Taylor, and he tackled me side-on. My studs got caught along the ground, and my knee collapsed inwards. I knew straight away I was in serious trouble. I had just put a shoulder injury behind me, I was back and in really good shape and I'd worked hard in pre-season. For that to happen was a cruel blow, so hard to take.

'I knew straight away I was in serious trouble': Kirsty Peacock, Munster physiotherapist, attends to Alan Quinlan, who ruptured his cruciate ligament against Sale

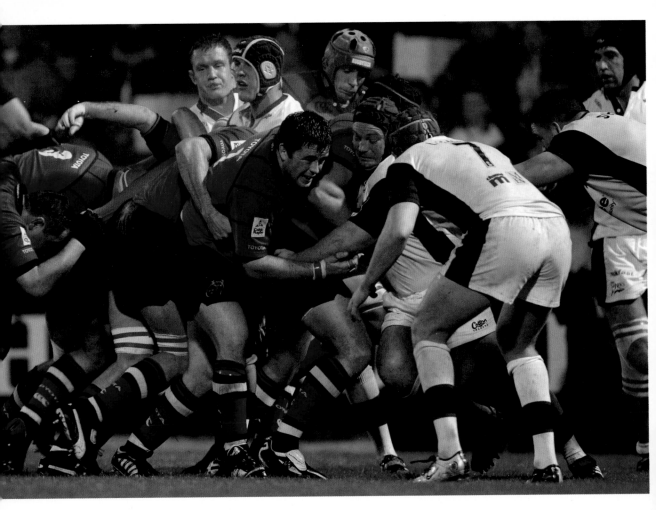

Marcus Horan lends his weight to the maul

I was brought into the dressing room by our doctor, Tadhg O'Sullivan. He knew – the look on his face wasn't good. There was too much movement in my knee. So he left me for a few minutes on my own, and to be honest it was a lonely, sad time for me. I just didn't know where my career was going. For the next fifteen minutes I just sat there and cried. Cried afterwards as well. And the next day. The hardest phone call of all was to my mother. She was at the game. I told her I wasn't too bad, that we'd know tomorrow after the scan. We got off the plane, and Rog brought me to his house. He was brilliant to me, stayed with me right through the scan the next day. The scan showed I had ruptured my cruciate ligament and damaged my medial ligaments, badly. I was going to be out of action for six or seven months. Even if we got to the final, I wasn't going to stand much chance of being fit in time.

> **WE HAD SEVEN AGAINST EIGHT IN A SCRUM, AND THEY WERE GOING FOR A NUDGE, BUT WE WHEELED THEM AND WE GOT THE PUT-IN. BUT WE RESET STRAIGHT AWAY. TOO MUCH YOUTHFUL ENTHUSIASM. THEY GET THE NUDGE ON OUR SCRUM, THE BALL SQUIRTS OUT AND THEY SCORE. WE WERE JUST TOO HONEST.**

DAVID WALLACE: The previous year had been a bad one for me, form-wise. I started the new season all guns blazing, not wanting to have a repeat of it. Then I got injured two weeks before the Sale game and I was only on the bench for that. I was starting to think, 'Here we go again.' Even when Quinny was injured, I wasn't brought on. I'm sitting there waiting for the call, then I'm told I'm not going on. No disrespect to Trevor Hogan, but when the guy in your position goes down, you expect to get on.

DECLAN KIDNEY: It was a miserable night. Frankie Sheahan had scored a try for us in the first half, and we were playing well. Everything was happening around the sides of the rucks and mauls. The ball wasn't being pushed out wide – there was very little chance to do anything with it. That was my logic for the substitution. But it's hard to justify it to fellas, because they want it so much and their work ethic is so good.

JERRY FLANNERY: Frankie got binned early in the second half, and I came on. Then he got injured, and I was on again. I was up against some of the best players that the Premiership had to offer and I thought I was doing OK.

DECLAN KIDNEY: After about an hour we were leading by a point but we were down to fourteen. We had seven against eight in a scrum, and they were going for a nudge, but we wheeled them and we got the put-in. But we reset straight away. Too much youthful enthusiasm. They get the nudge on our scrum, the ball squirts out and they score. We

Shaun Payne tries to break a Sale tackle

were just too honest. I would never give out about that because that is the nature of the team. It's innate in them. The second error came when we were trying to win the game, and not hang on for a bonus point. If you stick to being honest, it'll go for you more often than it'll go against you.

SHAUN PAYNE: Back in the changing rooms everyone was very down. We were all squeezed in there on these blue benches, the team and the reserves. Nobody said a word for a long time. Then Puccy tried to apologize for something he had done but straight away the boys said, 'No, no, no – we're a team and we lose as a team.' The lads wouldn't stand for somebody taking the blame for a match.

Deccie got up and said, 'It's not over. It's nowhere near over.' We hadn't played that badly, the bounce of the ball had gone against us once or twice. There was still a long way to go, but we had five matches left and we knew we had to win the lot.

DONNCHA O'CALLAGHAN: We came away from that game, and some people were writing us off, saying we'd be lucky to get out of the group. I was thinking, 'I like the sounds of this.' We love being backed into a corner. It shouldn't be the way it has to be, and we have to have to move on from that. But at that stage of the season it was a kick up the ass that we all needed.

JERRY FLANNERY: A week is a long time in rugby. After that match Kirsty [Peacock, physiotherapist] said to me, 'Frankie could be in a bit of trouble, you might be starting next week.' I'd been training with some of the best players in Europe, week in and week out, and I never felt, 'I'm out of my depth here.' I just thought, 'Jesus, I'd love to play, I think I could do a good job.' I was just waiting. Waiting to get a chance. I always had an awful lot of self-belief. I wouldn't have been able to go in there and train for all that time while not getting a game if I didn't. I was thinking about it all week, thinking about the Castres hooker and how I wanted to smash him, dominate him.

FRANKIE SHEAHAN: I'd hurt my neck in the first scrum, but it didn't feel that bad, and I played on. The scan showed some problems, but there was never a suggestion that it was going to finish my season. They sent me to Germany to see the top guy in the world, and he cleared me, but I came back, and they didn't agree with him. It kept dragging on. Four weeks. Six weeks. Eight. I kept latching on to the hope that I'd be back before the end of the season.

ANTHONY FOLEY: The following week we beat Castres at Thomond Park and we played well. We kept ourselves alive and scored five tries. Jerry Flannery got one of them – he had a big game. There was a break then for the autumn internationals. Ireland

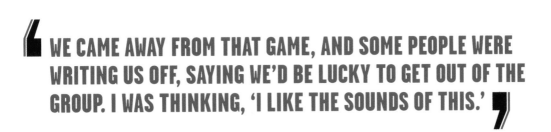

❝ WE CAME AWAY FROM THAT GAME, AND SOME PEOPLE WERE WRITING US OFF, SAYING WE'D BE LUCKY TO GET OUT OF THE GROUP. I WAS THINKING, 'I LIKE THE SOUNDS OF THIS.' ❞

were playing New Zealand first. It was being reported that I was going to be captain, but I had been told I wasn't going to be in the twenty-two if Simon Easterby was passed fit. If he didn't make it, I would be captain – so that was a bit of a head-wrecker.

CHARLIE MULQUEEN, *IRISH EXAMINER*: Anthony Foley must have cut a forlorn figure as he made his way down the N7 and on to Killaloe last night. He had just been omitted from the Irish team to tackle New Zealand at Lansdowne Road on Saturday and deprived of the opportunity of following in the footsteps of his father Brendan in forming the first father-and-son combination to put one over on the All Blacks. Brendan, of course, did it for Munster in 1978; the likelihood now is that Anthony won't have that chance again.

ANTHONY FOLEY: It was tough. It took me a while to get over it. But, you know, put that into the bitterness bank. It will serve its purpose at another time. My season was all about Munster then, the way it turned out. I'd loved to have played a game there and then and got a bit of that anger out. But I knew it would come out, in due course.

Opposite: Trevor Halstead fights through two Castres
tacklers en route to touching down for a try

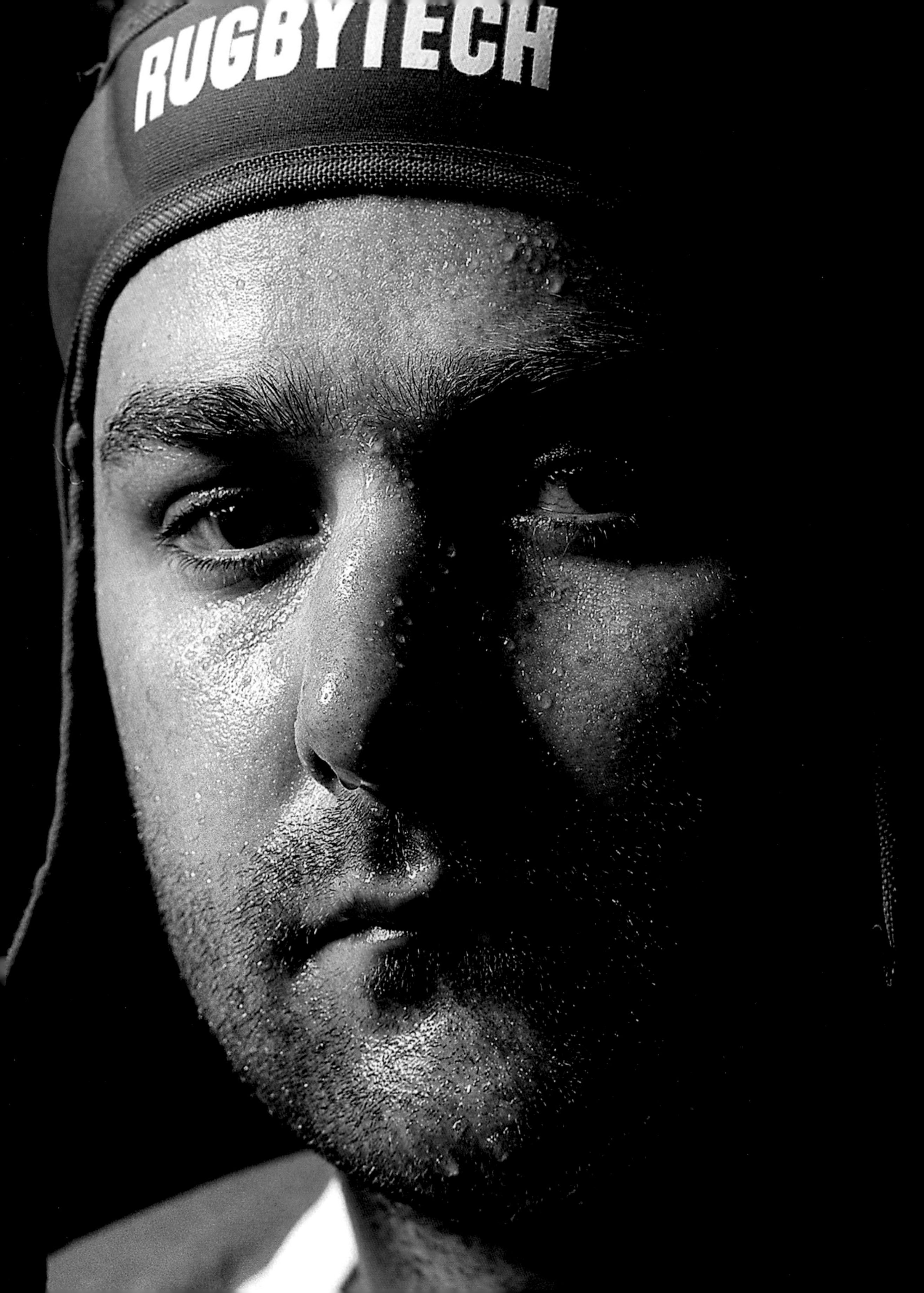
RUGBYTECH

CHAPTER 9

ANTHONY FOLEY'S STORY

❝ PLAY WITH BITTERNESS AND PRIDE –
BE PROUD OF WHERE YOU COME FROM ❞

Rugby is basically a street fight with a ball. You have many ways to score but sometimes the shortest route is straight over a fella. Sometimes you need to run at people rather than around them – you need to put a bit of manners on them.

Once you go into that arena, fifteen against fifteen, it's about making the other side take a backward step, putting them into retreat. It's about other things, too. Can you be cuter than them? Can you lull them into a false sense of security, set them up for a fall? You can go about it in many ways, like a chess player. There are big psychological battles going on out there. A man with a strong will and a good mind can beat a man who's faster and more muscular. You can intimidate a guy if you're in his face the whole time and you never let him see that you're tired. Just let him know early, make sure he gets the message that you're going to be around all day, that you're never going to let up. Stand tall and show them nothing. No weakness.

My father is Brendan Foley. He played for Munster and Ireland, but mostly he played for Shannon. As a small boy I was sent to the games with him, maybe to make sure he'd come home at a reasonable hour. That wasn't always the case – I'd end up asleep under jackets in Cowhey's pub.

I carried his bag into the changing rooms at Thomond Park and I minded the spot where he used to tog out – I was very protective of it. One day Ger McMahon threw his jacket on the hook in that corner, just to rise me. I said, 'That's my father's place!' I tog out in that spot myself now.

Sometimes there were other young lads around, other sons of the Shannon players,

> ## ONCE YOU GO INTO THAT ARENA, FIFTEEN AGAINST FIFTEEN, IT'S ABOUT MAKING THE OTHER SIDE TAKE A BACKWARD STEP, PUTTING THEM INTO RETREAT.

and we'd play our own little game at the end, three a side, the full length of the pitch. Knackered by the end of it, but very happy.

I went to school at St Munchin's in Limerick – a rugby school. We got to the final of the Munster Schools Senior Cup and lost to Pres. Not winning that match is one of my greatest regrets. They were very well organized, coached by some fellow called Kidney. Munchin's hadn't won the cup in ten years, and it was one of those occasions that got away from us. When you're not fully prepared mentally for a game like that, it can slip away.

When I made the Munster Under-20s team we had a forwards coach called Dan Mooney, a Young Munster man. Ulster had a lot of highly rated players, but he told us nobody had the divine right to beat us just because of who they were. He told us to go out there and play with bitterness and pride – to be proud of where we came from. We fought tooth and nail for one another and we beat them. Then we beat Leinster and Connacht. When you stick together you're an awful lot stronger. Dan Mooney doesn't coach any more, which is a pity for the younger players.

I got capped when I was twenty-one. I'd come through the ranks, played on the underage teams. For the first time in my life I set myself goals, and one of them was getting to the 1995 World Cup. I did that – and then it went downhill for me. Nobody prepares you for the year after you get your first cap – everybody assumes that you'll kick on, but there's still a lot of learning to be done. Looking back, if I knew then what I know now I'd hit myself a slap across the jaw to wake myself up. I was playing with injuries, limping around the pitch, and I wasn't looking after myself properly. I got six caps in my first year and for the four years after that I got a total of three. Somebody should have caught me by the throat and told me to cop on. I got back in around the time when the whole Munster thing took off.

These days I try to make sure that we're all going in the one direction at Munster, that there are no cliques or hidden agendas or in-house bullying, that the new guys buy into the bitterness and pride aspect.

The way I look at it, it's a big moment in your life to be in the Munster squad, and I try to make sure fellows appreciate that, so when they do earn the right to wear the jersey they don't do a half-arsed job of it. A lot of fellows in our squad can't wait to get to Munster training. They love being in the changing room and meeting the lads for a beer and a bit of crack. At the end of the day we really enjoy each other's company, and that can be seen by the way we treat each other on the pitch.

If I'm going to be remembered I'd like to be seen as a stubborn player, somebody who wouldn't give in. There were times during my career when I could have called it quits and gone off and done other things, but there was always a goal there, always something to achieve. Once there's something to chase, I'll chase it.

CHAPTER 10
DAD'S ARMY ON THE MARCH

❝ OH THAT DIDN'T GO DOWN WELL. ❞

Six weeks after the victory against Castres, Munster travelled to Rodney Parade, Newport, to take on the Dragons in their third match of the European campaign. For reasons best known to themselves, two of the Newport players chose to fire off a couple of rounds of live ammunition in the press three days before kick-off. The Dragons had been walloped at home by Sale in their previous outing, but that beating did nothing to spike the guns of the intrepid twosome.

'They're an ageing side,' said the 23-year-old prop Rhys Thomas. 'It's probably one of the weakest Munster sides. It's dangerous to say, but I think it's a great opportunity for us.' His colleague in the backline, Ceri Sweeney, offered the further opinion that the Munster half-backs, Ronan O'Gara and Peter Stringer, 'can both be intimidated'.

SHAUN PAYNE: Oh that didn't go down well. That spurred us on big-time. They were calling us a bunch of geriatrics. Not a very clever thing to say to a team that thrives on the putdown. We were never going to fight that one in the press, I can guarantee you. But that's not to say we weren't going to fight it. We went over there and won well. Some people were saying we should have got a bonus point, but we had to win to stay in the tournament and we were happy.

DECLAN KIDNEY: Unless things have changed drastically, any way win in Europe is a good win. I thought people were getting above themselves talking about bonus points. It was the same thing when we beat them at Thomond Park the following week. People

New kid Jerry Flannery carries for 'ageing' Munster against Dragons at Rodney Parade, Newport

talking about us not getting a bonus point, but with twelve minutes left we were behind in that game.

DENIS LEAMY: Certain newspaper people were very happy to write us off after that. We were a finished team, over the hill, Dad's Army. It was laughable.

ANTHONY FOLEY: We always say, 'We'll get the first four bonus points first and if there's one more to come after it, well and good. Sometimes we walk into the press conference afterwards, and everybody has the benefit of hindsight. 'You didn't get the four tries – are you disappointed?' You've to be out on the pitch to understand that to beat most sides in Europe takes a lot of hard work. You never go out and say, 'OK, we're going to get five points here.' Because they're the days you get turned over. We know from experience that there's no point in getting too carried away, that if you can leave yourself with something to do in the last game everything is possible.

Opposite: And the old-timers pitch in, too: John Hayes (top) and John Kelly

Mick O'Driscoll, who filled in effectively for the injured Paul O'Connell in the latter months of 2005, looks to unload in the home victory over Dragons

Ten days later, on 27 December, Paul O'Connell returned to the side for a Celtic League match against Connacht, after being out for three months with a hand injury. Rested and in superb physical shape, O'Connell was about to strike the best form of his career. No team in world rugby would not be improved by having O'Connell in it, but in his absence Mick O'Driscoll had been barnstormingly effective. Back with Munster after two years at Perpignan, O'Driscoll was having a big season.

For David Wallace, life was good. Twenty-four minutes after being left on the bench at Sale when Alan Quinlan suffered his injury, Wallace was sent into the fray and never looked back. He would be the Munster and Ireland Number 7 for the rest of the season. The unfortunate Frankie Sheahan was still battling against his neck injury, and in his absence Jerry Flannery was seizing his chance, after wondering if it would ever come. For him, an international career beckoned. Christian Cullen had not played in ten months, after suffering another shoulder injury, but was beginning to see light at the end of a very dark tunnel.

In the centre Trevor Halstead had yet to hit form, Rob Henderson was in the wilderness, the rugby league veteran Gary Connolly had been tried at Number 13, and the homegrown Barry Murphy was waiting for his chance. There were other tyros sniping around the edge of the team. Like Flannery, the robust wing Ian Dowling had begun the season in the All Ireland League with Shannon. He had yet to make the Munster bench in Europe, but by Christmas he was coming up fast on the rails.

Trevor Halstead: on the brink of a fine run of form

The bench for Heineken Cup days was taking on a familiar look, and was not short on quality. The seasoned Federico Pucciariello and the young hooker Denis Fogarty covered the front row, the lock Trevor Hogan had already been capped, and Stephen Keogh was a formidable option in the back row. The 21-year-old Kiwi Jeremy Manning had edged ahead of the evergreen Paul Burke as cover to Ronan O'Gara, and the versatile Tomas O'Leary was the stand-in scrum-half.

On New Year's Eve, Munster were in Dublin to take on Leinster in a Celtic League match that packed the RDS. Leinster, sparked by Felipe Contepomi's electric running game at Number 10, were a team on the up. Munster had given them a beating earlier in the season, but they had learned from it.

Kidney pitched Barry Murphy into the centre against Brian O'Driscoll. At Munster's team meeting, the coach said his piece, and the message was reinforced by the usual suspects; Foley, O'Connell, John Kelly. They had to be precise in everything they did; Leinster's lethal backline had to be deprived of quality ball, and so on. Then O'Connell said, 'Ah, I think Quinny has something to say.'

Alan Quinlan was in civvies at the back of the room. He was a long, long way from being fit, but he could contribute in other ways.

'I know,' he said, 'that what everyone has said is right, like. We'll have to be precise, we'll have to protect the ball and hold possession. But, boys, if we want to beat these fellas, we'll just have to get out there and smash 'em. Simple as that.'

Leinster, though, did not stand still long enough to be smashed. Contepomi scored two tries and twenty-five points, and his team won 35–23. For the subdued O'Gara, there were unflattering comparisons with the Argentinian playmaker in the press. The defeat hurt Munster and convinced some that they were on the road to nowhere, that the baton in Ireland was passing to the boys in blue.

TONY WARD, *IRISH INDEPENDENT*: Munster's inadequacies behind the scrum have become an embarrassment in the professional age. Only now is the absence of Mike Mullins being fully appreciated. Shaun Payne offers the only semblance of guile or craft but at full-back he is too isolated to exact any meaningful influence. Qualification for the quarter-finals of the Heineken Cup can still be achieved. But beyond that, forget it. This Munster side is a one-trick forward pony serviced by quality at half-back alone.

CHARLIE MULQUEEN, *IRISH EXAMINER*: Leinster can now fairly claim to be the top side in the country. No amount of spin will camouflage the Munster shortcomings, and unless something radical happens quickly, then their season could be as good as over in another three weeks.

BARRY MURPHY: I was marking Brian O'Driscoll and I thought I was doing pretty well. Then, with about ten minutes left, I got a pass from Ronan and I was clean through but I didn't know it – I threw a pass out to John Kelly. I probably saw the headlines. I should have backed myself but I literally froze. Two minutes later Ronan threw out another pass, and I dropped it. Nightmare.

RONAN O'GARA: It was reported after that game that my body language was all wrong, that I was ill-tempered, foul-mouthed and I fought with my team-mates. I didn't play well, but fighting with my team-mates? I don't do that. Sometimes there are differences of opinion, but it's all about what's best for the team.

ANTHONY FOLEY: They got a couple of tries near the end that took them away from us and made their score a bit flattering. Then their out-half went into the crowd with his hands behind his ears. So that was noted.

DECLAN KIDNEY: There had been a dip in form, but you can't play well for the whole season. I knew the character of the team and I knew they would come back. The

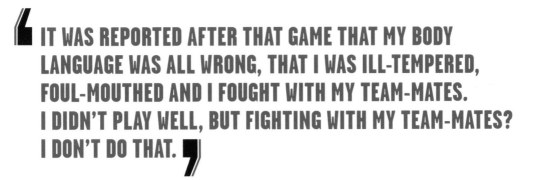

❝ IT WAS REPORTED AFTER THAT GAME THAT MY BODY LANGUAGE WAS ALL WRONG, THAT I WAS ILL-TEMPERED, FOUL-MOUTHED AND I FOUGHT WITH MY TEAM-MATES. I DIDN'T PLAY WELL, BUT FIGHTING WITH MY TEAM-MATES? I DON'T DO THAT. ❞

following week we went to Edinburgh and we really started to play a bit of rugby that night. I got the feel that things were turning for us.

IAN DOWLING: I got picked against Edinburgh, and we were a point up in the last minute when I gave away a penalty. It was a horrible moment. I just turned my back on Chris Paterson and hoped to God he'd miss. He missed. I wasn't really expecting to be involved against Castres after that because I'd never played in the Heineken Cup, but Deccie put his trust in me. That gave me even more confidence.

DECLAN KIDNEY: Leaving Anthony Horgan out for Castres was tough. He got a fair shellacking after the All Blacks match in November. He had lost a bit of form and he had some work to do. I said, 'What can I do?' and he said, 'There's nothing you can do – I've got to do it myself.' He went away and played with Cork Con and that wasn't easy.

ANTHONY HORGAN: I was obviously overjoyed to be picked against New Zealand, but at the back of my mind was the thought, 'Is this a good one to be playing?' They were coming off the back of their demolition of the Lions. I got a slating after it and to be honest I took a dip in form and confidence.

DECLAN KIDNEY: Before the Castres match this fax came in, and I read it out to the lads. It was about how a ship can look great in its own harbour, but every so often it has to leave shore and it can encounter rough waters. The ship has to be able to go through that. For us, the south of France is the hardest place to go to and deliver. Our record at Thomond Park speaks for itself, but it was all on the line down there. Again. I said, 'Lads, we know what we're facing. This is going to be rough here tonight.'

DONNCHA O'CALLAGHAN: We've played Castres an awful lot, and stuff goes on. Little incidents you don't forget. I'd been in a few scraps at Thomond Park in the first match and I knew I was going to get it back tenfold. I remember some prop coming on and scrabbing the face off me – Leamy is still slagging me over it. Stephen Keogh came on as a sub that day, and I owe him one over that. I'm getting the head flaked off me, and in the middle of that we get a penalty. Instead of bailing in and helping me out, he taps

Opposite: **Paul O'Connell, back from injury, in imperious form against Castres**

and goes – heads away off. I said to him afterwards, 'Thanks for watching my back there!' But I couldn't fault him really – he had to make an impression while he was on the pitch. Going down there, I knew they weren't going to give it up easily.

SHAUN PAYNE: First half, we really put them to the sword. I know we scored most of our points in the second half but we did the real damage early on. And the crucial thing was that, after getting two tries in the first half, we came out after half-time and just blitzed them straight away. They were gone after that. You could see they weren't interested. Getting a bonus point there was huge. Our tails were really up, and we started believing we could really top this group.

PETER STRINGER: It was the first time all season that the team clicked as a unit. All the talk about the backs not being up to much – it does play on your mind. It was a good hammering, 46–9, and guys were having a go from all over the pitch.

BARRY MURPHY: Rog was on top form that night. He was throwing out passes I'd never had in my life, inviting me to run on to the ball. That's exactly how I like to play. After that, we couldn't wait to have a crack at Sale. It was history repeating itself – the best team in England coming to Thomond Park in the last match of the pool.

TREVOR HALSTEAD: I was feeling the pressure. I'd hate to have had it hanging over my head – losing at Thomond Park in my first season. We needed a bonus point to top the pool ahead of Sale, but for me it was all about the unbeaten record.

IAN DOWLING: It was my first time getting to wear the red of Munster in Thomond Park. They put me in a room with Rog the night before – I'd say the management thought I was going to freak out or something. When I got to the ground and saw all the supporters there it sent a shiver down my spine. Then I heard my name being shouted out from the crowd. It was absolute bedlam.

MICK CLEARY, *DAILY TELEGRAPH*: Sale are taking on more than a mere team in Limerick this evening. They will have to battle myths and legends, intangible factors that swirl

Opposite top: Barry Murphy, who made his first-team debut in the Celtic League defeat to Leinster, in action against Castres Opposite bottom: Bring on Sale: Stephen Keogh, Mick O'Driscoll and Shaun Payne after beating Castres

Paul O'Connell runs out at Thomond Park for the final group-stage match, against Sale

around the concrete, run-down stadium on the edge of the old garrison town. Munster have not lost a Heineken Cup tie at Thomond Park. Ever. That's twenty-two matches and counting. Victory would establish Sale as a force in their own right for ever and a day. They would have punctured that Thomond aura of invincibility and shown themselves to be champions-in-waiting. Tickets were trading on eBay yesterday for £500 a pair. Sounds a bargain.

GERRY THORNLEY, *THE IRISH TIMES*: Sale are a crack outfit, as good as any Munster have put to the sword at their Limerick fortress. On such a seismic occasion Sebastien Chabal's first rumble, and the first tackle on him, is likely to be seminal.

RONAN O'GARA: It was the best atmosphere I've ever played in, better than any international. The passion of the crowd was incredible. I knew we were going to win that game

Opposite: 'I wouldn't say it was a case of, "Kick it to Chabal and we'll bust him" – that was just the way it turned out'

Sale's Jason Robinson gets a grip on Barry Murphy's foot, but it wasn't enough to prevent the Munster man touching down for a try 'out of nowhere'

before we kicked off. I just knew it. It wasn't anything to do with us. It was the fact that a few people on their team thought they knew what was coming, but you never know. You just think you do.

PAUL O'CONNELL: Early in the first half, after a penalty for them, there was a great restart by Rog. I charged after it and when I was halfway there I could see that Chabal was going to be under it. I wouldn't say it was a case of, 'Kick it to Chabal and we'll bust him' – that was just the way it turned out. Sometimes you need that bit of luck – you need the force to be with you. The ball hung in the air, and I had to slow up a little bit, before he caught it. Then I hit him. He tried to keep his feet – it was the male pride, he didn't want to go to ground – and then the boys all came piling in behind me. We had him held up and he should have been fighting to get on to the ground, but his strength came against him. He didn't want to go to ground, he wanted to retain the ball. Fair

> **THE MORE TEAMS DON'T FOCUS ON OUR BACKLINE, THE MORE I LIKE IT BECAUSE WE CAN CATCH THEM ON THE HOP. AND THAT'S WHAT HAPPENED NEXT.**

play to him, he did retain it, but the more he tried to stay on his feet, the further back he went until eventually he hit the deck. The crowd were going mad at this stage.

A while after that, Rog and Axel made a great double hit on him, and that got another big roar. Then he came around the corner at one stage and did a chip ahead and collected it. Now, in fairness – a chip ahead? When you're that type of player and you're doing chip aheads you've got to wonder what's going on in his head.

DECLAN KIDNEY: The hit on Chabal was like one of those moments where all of a sudden you get a two-yard nudge in the scrum. Only better. It had a huge effect on the team. You could see them thinking, 'Right, that's set the standard.'

SHAUN PAYNE: The forwards drove Axel over for our first try, then the backs put a move together, and Dowls scored in the corner. Two tries in the bag and plenty of time left. I've got no problem whatsoever with our pack always been talked up – we genuinely do have an outstanding pack. But the more teams don't focus on our backline, the more I like it because we can catch them on the hop. And that's what happened next.

BARRY MURPHY: There was a lineout, a couple of rucks, and we were being driven back, so Ronan just tried to clear his lines from the halfway line. Myself and Ian were the only ones outside him. I took off early so I could chase the kick and put a bit of pressure on them. As I was running, I was looking around – I didn't know where the ball was. Then it just dropped into my arms. I think it rebounded off one of their players. Donners was on my right, Ian was on my left – I was just trying to pass. That's the first option for me, always. I don't have the same strength to go through tackles as Trevor or Ian. The lads kept their defenders occupied, and when I got into the twenty-two I was

HE'S GOT SOME GAS. TO SCORE A TRY LIKE THAT, OUT OF NOWHERE, WAS A DREAM. WE USUALLY HAVE TO WORK SO HARD FOR OUR SCORES. TO HAVE A FELLA WHO MAKES IT HAPPEN LIKE THAT IS BRILLIANT.

motoring because I had taken off so fast. I just backed myself, kept going and crashed over the line. I looked up, and my buddies were all in front of me, hanging over the barriers. Cathal Garvey and Garrett Noonan and my girlfriend, Louise Ryan. They were the first people I saw. Then Ian and Rog jumped in on top of me. The weight of Ian's big arse nearly broke my back. I started roaring and Rog was like, 'Get off his back!'

JERRY FLANNERY: He's got some gas. To score a try like that, out of nowhere, was a dream. We usually have to work so hard for our scores. To have a fella who makes it happen like that is brilliant. For Munster to go out and sign a player who can do what Baz can do would cost massive money. And you could be getting a superstar who doesn't buy into what we have here. Plus, he's a Munchin's man and he's Limerick born and bred. It was turning out to be a fabulous combination, Trevor and Baz. Trevor was really coming good for us too.

ANTHONY FOLEY: In the first half we blew them away, and when they came out after half-time they were playing to make sure we didn't get the bonus point. They just kept pinning us back, like a side trying to hold on to a lead of some sort. We couldn't get into any good attacking positions. Then, when it looked like they might hang on, Wally popped up.

DAVID WALLACE: In injury time they let their guard down and we got down into their half. We were getting closer to their line, Shaun made a great break, and for me it was just a case of getting to that breakdown. I picked the ball and I couldn't believe there was nobody on the right-hand side. I just snuck in. Ah, Jesus, it was a great moment, in

Opposite: Ian Dowling after the final whistle

fairness. That was game over then. Bonus point, top of the pool. The place erupted, and when we eventually got into the dressing room the crowd called us back out. Axel said a few words. We didn't want to make a big deal out of it. You want to show your appreciation but at the same time you don't want to be saying as a team, 'This is brilliant. We're celebrating now.'

ANTHONY FOLEY: We were sick and tired of laps of honour and waving at the crowd when we had nothing to show for it. We were dragged back out, and I was asked to say a few words. I don't like doing it, because you can say the wrong thing, something that somebody can use against you. So I kept it short and sweet and let everyone go home happy.

BARRY MURPHY: The next day we found out we'd be playing Perpignan in the quarter-final, at Lansdowne Road. I was on a high, I couldn't wait for it. On 3 March, we played Ulster on a Friday night, up in Belfast. I had changed my boots the week before. They had long studs and they hadn't been worn down a bit. I had trained all week in Limerick with them and they were fine, but the ground up there was harder. When I ran on the field I thought, 'Shit, these aren't right, the studs are too long.' But it was too late then.

Twenty minutes in I got hit by Andrew Maxwell and Jonny Bell, and my studs got caught in the ground. The pain was unbelievable. The bone was sticking out the side of my leg. I'd had broken bones before, but nothing hurt like this. The stretcher came on, and Paul Burke and Trevor Halstead were on either side of it. I grabbed hold of their legs. They were trying to pull away but I wouldn't let go. I was roaring with the pain. Some Ulster fans started jeering me. It was horrible, the lowest feeling I've ever had.

They took me to the hospital, and my dad came with me. He'd been at the match. When I got there the nurses were going, 'It's not that bad at all! Just a sprain, I'd say. You'll be grand, love.' The morphine had kicked in, so I was thinking, 'Shit – am I after making a meal of this? I'm going to look like an unbelievable fool.'

The ankle had gone back in at this stage so I was saying to myself, 'OK, I must have imagined it.' I got a bit of a boost then, while they were taking me for an x-ray. The Perpignan match was in my head. Four weeks away. I might be fine. Next thing the nurse came back and she said, 'The surgeon will be here in minute now – but you've dislocated your ankle and broken your leg.'

I just went, 'Oh Jesus!' I broke down. She wheeled me out into the waiting room, and it was packed. Friday-night crowd. There were a couple of Ulster fans there. They were nice, trying to have the crack with me, but I broke down again, and my dad had to ask them to leave me to myself.

IT WAS TOUGH FOR BARRY, BECAUSE HE HAD MISSED THE WHOLE OF THE PREVIOUS SEASON WITH AN INJURY AND HE WAS FLYING. BUT HE'LL BE BACK.

We flew to Cork that night, and I had an operation on the Sunday. That was it. Season over.

DECLAN KIDNEY: It was tough for Barry, because he had missed the whole of the previous season with an injury and he was flying. But he'll be back. At that stage, our Ireland players were away for the Six Nations, and we weren't going to be together as a full squad for eight weeks. We knew the Perpignan match was going to be a war of attrition. That's the way they play their rugby.

JERRY FLANNERY: In any rugby match, but especially against a physical side like Perpignan, everything starts with the scrum, you know? And the cornerstone of the Munster pack is John Hayes. He never gets man of the match – actually, that's a cliché now. But if your tighthead is in trouble, nothing will work. If anything happened to John Hayes, we were going to be in serious shit.

CHAPTER 11
JOHN HAYES'S STORY

❝ I'D JUST LIKE TO BE SEEN AS AN HONEST, HARD PLAYER WHO GAVE HIS ALL. ❞

I don't know why they started calling me The Bull – must have had something to do with my farming background, I suppose. I don't mind it. I've been called a lot worse. My grandfather had this land before my father. He was John Hayes as well and he died a couple of years before I was born. We've 150 acres, not too bad, but in this day and age people have to start getting bigger farms.

I'm the second-eldest, and the oldest boy. There are four of us, and we all worked on the farm after school when we were young. We never had to be made do it. We did it because we wanted to and because we enjoyed it. I'd say I got my strength from my father, Mike. He's only five foot nine but he's very wide and blocky. He used to go round to sports meetings once a month throwing a 56 lb weight, just a lump of lead with a chain on it. Working on a farm, you develop natural strength.

Cappamore's a hurling parish. Rugby was unheard of here. I remember saying that when I was growing up, if you'd showed somebody a rugby ball, they'd have thought it was a football that had been rolled over by a car. The first game of rugby I was ever at, I played in it. I was nineteen.

My neighbour from up the road, John O'Dea, was playing for Bruff. He'd been telling me I should go up and play. I said, 'Yeah, I will I will I will.' But I was never going to turn up to some club on a Tuesday night and say, 'Here I am, I want to play rugby.' It's not that easy. I was never going to just walk in some place. John was twenty-five or twenty-six before he started. He was fair strong and he became a great prop for Bruff. One day I met him on the road, and he was going that night.

'Will you come?' he said.

'I will, so.'

I had no gear or nothing. Got a loan of togs and boots from him. I trained twice that week. Tuesday was fitness – there was no rugby at all, like, only all runnin'. On the Thursday then we started doing a bit of rugby, and that was the first time I ever held a rugby ball. I had a vague of idea of what it was about from looking at the television. On Sunday they were playing Newcastle West, and I don't know if they were stuck for numbers or something, but they asked me to play. I said, 'I will, yeah, no bother.' I didn't know the difference. Off I went and I ended up playing Number 6. It finished 0–0, so that says enough in itself, like. All I remember is running around the field, half-tackling fellas. I hadn't one fucking iota what I was doing. I was just running around the place. But I loved it. That's the one thing I can remember, thinking, 'Jesus, I can't wait to get back on Tuesday and start this again.'

When I was twenty-one I went to New Zealand on a working holiday. Once, there was no such thing – you either went there and never came back, or you didn't go. One or the other. But I wanted to go and see the world a bit. There was a Kiwi called Kynan McGregor playing for Bruff and he was heading home, so a couple of months later I went out after him and joined his club, Marist in Invercargill.

Around the same time, lifting started coming into the lineouts, so all of a sudden I was out of date – to heavy to be lifted. The boys were saying, 'Front row could be the way to go for you,' so I said I'd give it a go. In my first game as a prop I played loosehead and I got turned inside out. I hadn't a clue. All my neck muscles were stretched. But, sure, I learned. I'm at it since, anyway.

Some people will look at a scrum and they'll tell you it's just a way of restarting the game. But a scrum is the one time when it's eight on eight, where you literally just lock horns. It's about quality ball for the backs, but it's also trying to get stuck into the opposite pack, to dominate them for the day. Once you get off the mark and you meet it head on, you don't even feel it. If you hit it right you're fine, but if you're slow off the mark it can hurt.

Lifting came naturally enough to me – there's no big secret, just practice. To win a lineout, four people have to get the timing right. The fella throwing the ball, two fellas lifting and the fella jumping. That's all it is, practice. Just keep doin' 'em. Paul and Donncha are obsessed with getting it right and they don't make mistakes. They're both so tall and springy, it's easy to lift 'em.

> ## SOME PEOPLE WILL LOOK AT A SCRUM AND THEY'LL TELL YOU IT'S JUST A WAY OF RESTARTING THE GAME. BUT A SCRUM IS THE ONE TIME WHEN IT'S EIGHT ON EIGHT, WHERE YOU LITERALLY JUST LOCK HORNS.

I was a welder in Sixmilebridge when I started playing for Munster, back in '98. It took off from there for me, and I got capped two years later. Nowadays, a lot of fellas from Cappamore are playing underage rugby. People come over to my mother and father in the shop and start talking about it. Sometimes it's the talk of the place.

Criticism doesn't hurt me because I don't read it or listen to it. Sometimes people might say it to you, and that's the only way you'd know about it. I don't read the newspapers. I don't like hearing what people are saying about us, good or bad. I like to have my own focus and prepare in my own way. I'd just like to be seen as an honest, hard player who gave his all.

CHAPTER 12

LOSING A FRIEND, WINNING A WAR

> **I'M GOING TO HAVE TO CALM DOWN AND GET HOLD OF MYSELF HERE.**

In the third week of March, an Ireland side with nine Munster players won the Triple Crown at Twickenham. With Leinster also in the last eight of the Heineken Cup and the Irish provinces dominating the Celtic League, the game in Ireland had never been in better shape.

Ten days before the Perpignan match, the Munster squad was shocked by the tragic death of Conrad O'Sullivan, the 25-year-old Cork Constitution centre who had made several appearances in the Celtic League the previous season. A talented player, and an exceptionally popular young man, he had long been a close friend of several members of the squad.

DECLAN KIDNEY: Conrad was a pupil with me at Pres. He was a role model, as nice a young man as you could meet. The lads who played on different teams with him were down at his house when they brought him home before the funeral service started. To see the photographs all around the house was heartbreaking – pictures of him with the other lads playing for Munster Schools, Ireland Schools, different Munster teams.

His funeral took place on the wettest, wildest day imaginable. The cemetery was on the top of a hill. The lads were drenched to the skin in their suits, but they didn't feel anything. They only had thoughts for Conrad. They were people then, not rugby players. All of us are people first, and so many things happen around us. Over the course of a season, people close to us die and children are born. Real-life events.

> **HIS FUNERAL TOOK PLACE ON THE WETTEST, WILDEST DAY IMAGINABLE. THE CEMETERY WAS ON THE TOP OF A HILL. THE LADS WERE DRENCHED TO THE SKIN IN THEIR SUITS, BUT THEY DIDN'T FEEL ANYTHING. THEY ONLY HAD THOUGHTS FOR CONRAD.**

We're all with Munster for a short period of time, and if you can face the players at the end of it, after all the ups and downs, you'll have done OK for them.

DENIS LEAMY: I never got such a shock in all my life, walking into his house and seeing him there. It's unbelievable, even now, to think he's gone. We made our debuts for Munster the same day, we played in all the underage teams together. You think you'll be playing with this guy for Munster and Ireland for the rest of your career. I spoke to Declan a couple of days afterwards and told him how I was feeling. Looking back, I don't think I was mentally right for the Perpignan match.

DECLAN KIDNEY: On the Tuesday before Perpignan, we played a match in training on the back pitch at Thomond that was ruthless. Nobody held anything back. At half-time, a few of the lads were saying, 'This is crazy, we're getting nothing out of this.' But Mick O'Driscoll and Anthony Foley said, 'This is exactly what we're going to be coming up against. Exactly. They'll be climbing all over us.' Then the guys who had their doubts turned to me.

'Are you saying that we don't hold anything back here?'

'That's up to you – you're trying to get ready for a match that is going to be seriously physical.'

There was a massive amount of adrenalin flowing, but nobody lost it. Some fellas took a lot of heavy knocks, but they didn't hold any grudges. At the end, they just said, 'Right, we've it done now. Bring them on.' When Perpignan came at us in those first fifteen minutes, that session stood to us.

The Munster and Perpignan squads observe a minute's silence in memory of Conrad O'Sullivan before the quarter-final at Lansdowne Road

DENIS LEAMY: Coming up to the game I was very emotional. I wasn't sleeping. I had injured my ankle against England two weeks before, and that was wrecking my head as well. It was doubtful whether I would be able to pull through it. In the end I didn't. I was gone after twenty-five minutes. It was a strange day. The minute's silence and everything seemed to affect us.

DONNCHA O'CALLAGHAN: I didn't know Conrad as well as Denis or Stephen Keogh, but he was my friend, someone I always had fun with and who is badly missed. The minute's silence was toughest I've ever had to stand for. I was beside Rog and Leamy, and it was hard. That match wasn't the important thing that week. To be honest, I was glad when it was over.

ANTHONY FOLEY: It was a dog-fight – trench warfare. We hadn't played together for two months and we were very wary of them because we knew how good they were. They're

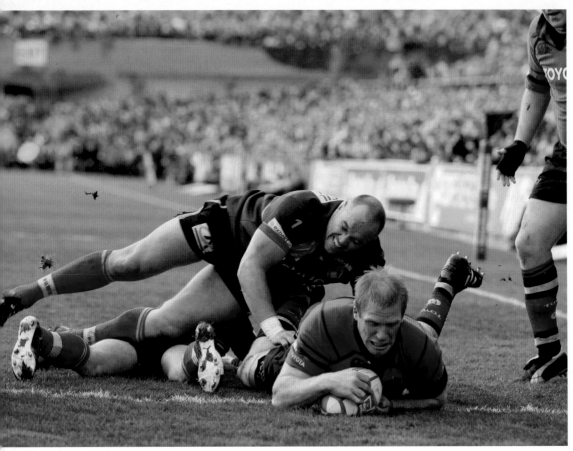
'Trench warfare': Paul O'Connell touches down for a try

dangerous and they're very passionate, and that mix can be very volatile. We had to make sure they were going to have nothing to fight for in the last few minutes.

ANTHONY HORGAN: I always knew I wasn't going to get picked for that game. You know by the way training goes, but you hold out a little bit of hope when the team is being announced. I was in the stand with my girlfriend, Jacqui, and a couple of friends. I found it very difficult, being up there and not part of it. I got to my seat and didn't feel right. I hung around for ten minutes and said, 'I'm going to the toilet.' I didn't come back.

I watched it on the screen at the Paddy Power stand out the back. There weren't that many people around, so I got away with it. I didn't worry about people noticing me because you can always get away with the excuse that you're going to the toilet. I texted Jacqui and told her I was watching it down below. She asked me if I wanted her to come down, but I said no, I'd rather be on my own. In my head I was thinking, 'The season is gone.' And standing out there watching it, I realized just how much I really

Opposite: **David Wallace breaks away**

❝ I WATCHED IT ON THE SCREEN AT THE PADDY POWER STAND OUT THE BACK. THERE WEREN'T THAT MANY PEOPLE AROUND, SO I GOT AWAY WITH IT. ❞

missed it. It was a difficult experience. I've been around these lads too long to wish anything other than good on them, but there is always going to be that little bit of bitterness, and anybody who tells you otherwise is not being honest. My feelings were complicated, but at the end of the day, deep down, you want what's best for the lads.

ROB HENDERSON: I hadn't played a single minute of rugby in nearly seven months and for most of that time I was fit to play – desperate to play. Then, out of the blue, I got called back on to the bench against Perpignan. I didn't get on, but for some reason I was in the frame again.

Back in September I got hauled ashore at half-time against Glasgow. I came on against Llanelli a week later and then it was off into the wilderness. I don't know what happened. I had trained hard but suddenly I was carved. You never think it's going to be you, and ultimately that made me think, 'Well, maybe this is my last season. Time to hang the boots up.' Physically I felt great, but mentally it was one too many knocks. When you're on the periphery it's difficult sometimes not to get upset.

The worst moment was against the Dragons over there, in December. I was on the bench and was told after about sixty minutes to go and warm up – I was going on. I warmed up for twenty minutes, and then the whistle blew. When you are anxious and dying for an opportunity to go and play rugby, you can see how that would hurt you.

Two weeks after Perpignan I got on the field for ten minutes against Edinburgh in Thomond Park. It was like you'd just won the raffle and you're running around like a headless chicken. Jesus Christ. One minute or eighty, I just enjoy playing the game. And not playing it is terrible. I've been around the block, but it was still tough.

DECLAN KIDNEY: When I came into the team room before the Perpignan match, the lads had been watching Leinster beating Toulouse and playing extremely well. That gave

Peter Stringer tries to disturb a Perpignan kick

our match an extra dimension – we were going to be up against Leinster at Lansdowne Road in the semi-final if we won. When we came through it [19–10], the hype started and didn't stop for three weeks.

BRENDAN FANNING, *SUNDAY INDEPENDENT*: It was when Shane Horgan crashed over at Le Stadium that the crowd back in Dublin, watching on the not-so-big screen at the back of the West Stand, began to salivate. Leinster would be coming home in triumph, and Munster would be waiting for them … There was just the small matter of sorting the Catalans. Munster kept their end of the bargain. It will be an interesting few weeks, leading to the biggest domestic day in the history of Irish rugby.

MARCUS HORAN: On the Tuesday after the Perpignan match we did a scrummaging session at Temple Hill and we went for a big push in the last scrum. All of a sudden I felt something in my calf – it was like being hit with a golf ball. I knew I was in trouble. Straight away I started thinking, 'How long will it take to get back?' This was nearly before I even hit the ground. I was panicking about the Leinster game straight away. Lying there, the next thing I thought was, 'God, will I even make the final?' Not being cocky, but should we get through.

You can't tell how bad things are until the swelling goes down and you get scanned. I was asking, 'When can I get the scan done? Can I get it done now?' They said, 'Look, you won't get scanned until tomorrow evening.' I couldn't drive home. Freddie [Pucciariello] drove my car home, and I sat in the back seat, with the leg up, ice stuck to it, feeling miserable.

My wife drove me out to the hospital, and I told her to go away then because I'd only be cranky. The scan showed it was a tear, but they couldn't tell how bad it was, so I was no better off. I had to wait and see how it settled down. Kirsty Peacock was great, and everything she said to do, I did. The first couple of days it felt fantastic – then I went off the drugs and the pain hit. I knew I had a battle on my hands. With a week and a half to go, I said, 'God I'm feeling good now – maybe I could do this. Deccie might give me a chance!' Then I trotted out on the Monday before the match and couldn't run. I had to call it. There was no chance.

DONNCHA O'CALLAGHAN: The build-up was ridiculous. I kept having to turn off the radio in the car and listen to CDs. All the time it was, 'We're giving away two tickets to the big game!' Everyone you met going down the road was on about it. I had a sleepless night on the Tuesday and I was thinking, 'This is crazy – the game isn't until Sunday.' I threw my dinner out on Wednesday night. I'd made a bit of fish and suddenly I got paranoid that I might get sick. It was sole and it looked absolutely fabulous, but I was looking at it, thinking, 'I'd better not chance it.' I ended up putting on a chicken breast and some pasta. I was getting worse. That night I was saying to myself, 'I'm going to have to calm down and get hold of myself here.'

WE WERE HEARING FROM PEOPLE ALL THE WAY THROUGH THE BUILD-UP, PEOPLE AT HOME TELLING US HOW IMPORTANT IT WAS THAT WE BEAT THEM, MUNSTER PEOPLE LIVING IN DUBLIN LETTING US KNOW WHAT IT FELT LIKE UP THERE. THEY WERE TELLING US THIS WAS MUCH MORE THAN JUST A RUGBY GAME – THIS WAS ABOUT WHAT THEY STOOD FOR AND WHAT IT WAS GOING TO BE LIKE FOR THEM WHEN THEY WENT TO WORK ON THE MONDAY.

PETER STRINGER: We were hearing from people all the way through the build-up, people at home telling us how important it was that we beat them, Munster people living in Dublin letting us know what it felt like up there. They were telling us this was much more than just a rugby game – this was about what they stood for and what it was going to be like for them when they went to work on the Monday. I never got such a sense of how, outside our group, a match can affect people's lives so much. It was non-stop hype for three weeks, and the match just seemed to get bigger and bigger the closer it got.

CHAPTER 13

TWO TRIBES

❝ THIS IS A DAY FOR MEN. ❞

At 1.20 p.m. on Sunday 23 April, in an upstairs room overlooking the splendid gardens at the rear of the Radisson hotel in Dublin, Anthony Foley rose to his feet. A light breeze was coming through the open windows, but the room was still warm. Outside it was the hottest day of the year so far. The Munster players, wearing tracksuits, were seated in front of Foley. Declan Kidney and the back-room staff were also present.

It is doubtful if any match in Irish rugby history generated as much hype as the one that was now an hour and forty minutes from kick-off. Venturing far beyond the usual clichéd territory – the rumble of Munster's forwards against the rapier thrust Leinster's backs – the media found some snappy talkers to suggest there was far more on the line than a place in the final of the Heineken Cup. This, said the sages, was a clash of cultures; rural Ireland against the big city, Barry's tea against grande skinny latte, cider against champagne.

Leinster were playing in their home city, and like Munster they had been given an allocation of 21,400 tickets, but they were about to find out that rumours of their burgeoning support were somewhat exaggerated. Somehow, perhaps because ultimately they wanted them far more, Munster fans got their hands on thousands of the Leinster tickets. One of the messages of goodwill sent to the Munster team, from the Garryowen man Willie Sexton, put it best: 'You have townlands, parishes, villages, towns, cities, the province and many more I know from around the globe willing you on. We know you'll do us proud once again.'

As usual, Foley found just the right words and delivered them with an intensity that moved everyone in the room. 'This is a day for men,' he said. 'It's a day when we have to stand up and be counted.'

DONNCHA O'CALLAGHAN: There's no point in pretending otherwise – there was a genuine fear there of how good Leinster were, what they were capable of if we allowed them to play. But when I looked around that room I could tell from guys' eyes, the way they were carrying themselves, that we were as right as we could possibly be.

PAT GERAGHTY: The goodwill towards the team was incredible, from the people in the hotel to the ground staff at Lansdowne Road. You'd get a pat on the shoulder from one, a covert wink from the other. On the journey to the ground the bus came in on the Merrion Road. I genuinely expected a sea of blue around the Dodder, but as we came by the RDS all you could see ahead was red. A mass of red. When we pulled up in the car park, the Sky TV lads were there, and as the players filed by towards the dressing room, Stuart Barnes said, 'My, they look serious.' And I said, 'Yeah, I think they're up for this one.'

ANTHONY HORGAN: I saw a hundred red shirts to every blue – I swear to God. It was an unbelievable sight. I was back in the team because Rags [John Kelly] had moved in to 13 and opened the door for me on the wing. I suppose I was lucky. Those of us who were there in 2000 and 2002, we always thought in the back of our heads that we'd get another chance at it. But time was moving on, and they were the favourites now, according to the bookies anyway.

RONAN O'GARA: I felt good. I felt fresh. I went out there before the lads for the warm-up, and the South Terrace was completely red. I put my tee on top of the padding beside the left-hand post and jogged around the goal-line. The crowd were giving me a massive cheer, and I was completely taken aback, because you never get that playing for Ireland at Lansdowne Road. It really put a spring in my step. The sun was shining, there wasn't too much wind and things couldn't have been better.

A lot of people were talking about Felipe Contepomi, and maybe there was a bit of bitterness in me over that. I felt they had short memories. I'd played him plenty of times over my career, and that day at the RDS, when they beat us, was probably one time that he got the better of me. I hated that day. I was raging, it made my blood boil. I couldn't wait to get a crack off him because a Celtic League match is one thing

THE CROWD WERE GIVING ME A MASSIVE CHEER, AND I WAS COMPLETELY TAKEN ABACK, BECAUSE YOU NEVER GET THAT PLAYING FOR IRELAND AT LANSDOWNE ROAD. IT REALLY PUT A SPRING IN MY STEP.

and a Heineken Cup semi-final is far different. I was confident in my own ability to perform.

DONNCHA O'CALLAGHAN: When we ran out there was an incredible cheer, our fans were everywhere, and I was thinking, 'Jesus, I thought the tickets were supposed to be fifty-fifty.'

DENIS LEAMY: It was tribal, like a Munster hurling final. And it was really tough. There was a great edge to it, incidents all over the place. Because there was so much pressure, you start doubting yourself in the run-up. But I always like to be a little bit nervous. Ronan had kicked us in front, and then we got another penalty which was in his range but we went for the corner. We backed ourselves. There was a brilliant take from Paulie in the lineout – even at that stage he was having an unbelievable game – and we drove it and I managed to get over for the try. It was some start for us.

ROB HENDERSON: Sitting on the bench, I was thinking, 'There's got to be a chance of me getting on here.' Then, after about twelve minutes, Rags hurts his shoulder and I'm going, 'Bollocks! Has anyone got the Dioralyte? I'm in all sorts of bother here.' Full-on old-school warm-up. Two stretches of the hamstrings, spit in the hands – right lads, I'm ready.

Fair play to Rog, we had a lineout on the left, and he called me into the game straight away. 'Go and smash someone,' he said. I took the ball in – and that's when I hurt my ankle. I was in pieces. I thought, 'Jesus, come on! You've waited all season for a match and you've lasted thirty-five seconds – you're not making love.' So I hobbled back to my feet, looked across, and there was Denis Hickie, flying along the left wing, ball in hand.

Overleaf: 'Jesus, I thought the tickets were supposed to be 50/50': Munster fans take over Lansdowne Road for the semi-final against Leinster

SHAUN PAYNE: I saw Paulie chasing him but – with all due respect – Paulie is no Linford Christie. I was quite far away, so I just made a beeline for the point where I thought I'd be able to get to him. Picked the spot and went for it. I could see he was heading for the outside and Denis is genuinely quick. Paulie didn't get too close to him, just forced him to run up the touchline. It's difficult coming in on the angle on a guy who's running that fast. If he had decided to step inside, there was no way I could have stopped myself. But I just managed to get him to put a foot in touch.

DECLAN KIDNEY: Games hinge on things like that. Had Denis got around us there, all of a sudden it was 10–7. That was the first time I thought, 'We could win this.' Somebody said it was brilliant to be a part of it – as long as you won. Very soon after that they kicked a ball deep in behind Anthony Horgan. I knew that was a pivotal moment for

Leinster out-half Felipe Contepomi, who had tormented Munster in the Celtic League, had a nightmare in the Heineken Cup semi-final

him. It was a real test. He got back to it and caught it. Denis half got him, but he fought his way out of it, got the ball away to Rog, and we managed to clear our lines. That was big for him. After what he had been through, it took moral courage.

DAVID LLEWELLYN, *INDEPENDENT*: Leinster's fly-half, Felipe Contepomi, had a nightmare with his kicking out of hand, even fluffing one of four restarts in the first half. Every time Leinster created a promising opening they would either spill the ball, pass it carelessly, knock it on, turn it over or give away a needless penalty.

ROB HENDERSON: The ankle was at me, but I got on with it. It wore off a little bit during the first half and myself and Trev shepherded the two boys in the middle [Brian O'Driscoll and Gordon D'Arcy] well. I don't think they threatened us at all. Rog kicked another couple of penalties and we went in at half-time 16–3 up. In the dressing room I had my foot strapped up to the hilt. I just said, 'Strap it as hard as you can, and I'll go for as long as I can.'

PETER JACKSON, *DAILY MAIL*: When O'Connell wasn't terrorizing them in the set-piece, he did so at times simply by standing there, his octopus-like presence enough for Leinster hooker Brian Blaney to be penalized for his crooked throwing rather than risk losing more by aiming it down the middle. Outplayed up front, Leinster found themselves smashed back at every turn they tried to take in their own backyard.

ROB HENDERSON: After about twenty-five minutes of the second half Girvan Dempsey made a break round the outside, and I scrag tackled him and then rolled the other way on the ankle. I couldn't stand on it. So I'm just roaring at someone to cover. Gordon D'Arcy is opposite me, looking at me, knowing that I've only got one leg. He's going, 'Gimme the ball! Gimme the ball! Look at him!' And I was shouting, 'Hayes! You're quicker, get out here. Just stand here.' Fortunately they didn't come that way. If he had come within arm's reach I would have tried to tackle him. Arm's reach and an inch, I'd never have got him.

I came off then and I will never, ever forget the standing ovation. Incredible feeling. I knew I'd never play there again. I started off at Kingston Rugby Club with two men and a dog watching. Few pints before the match, couple of fags at half-time and a rake of pints afterwards. To think that in fifteen years' time you will be clapped off by 50,000 to a standing ovation – I don't know. It meant a lot to me, that's all I can say.

They got it back to ten points, Freddie got binned, and it was a nervy time for us. Then all of a sudden Rog was bursting clear through and jumping into the crowd. He nearly missed the barrier. I would have laughed my socks off if he'd fallen over. He just about got over it. You knew we'd won the match when you saw Rog's deadpan grin. He's got a face full of teeth when he knows he's won. He's the same with cards. The teeth come out.

RONAN O'GARA: Afterwards I said that I jumped the hoarding in the heat of the moment, that if I could turn back the clock I wouldn't do it again. But, actually, I would – if I ever got a try of that magnitude. When emotions are high like that, whatever happens, happens.

DAVID WALLACE: Rog had been under a lot of pressure during the week and he really did feel it. In talking up Felipe they were kind of writing off Ronan. Scoring that try was just a great moment for him, but it was just the icing on the cake. He had a fantastic game from start to finish. But even then, we didn't let up. The scoreline was tough on them, and then Trevor made an interception and he had an empty pitch in front of him.

IAN DOWLING: He had 70 metres to run, and it seemed like there was quicksand along the middle of the pitch because he was going slower and slower.

SHAUN PAYNE: Big Trev, he's good over the first twenty. I'd say he was cursing himself for catching that ball. I watched him under the poles and he was ready to throw up after that. He was stuffed. He was gone. Gone.

ROB HENDERSON: The sniper rifles were out. As he was getting closer, I'm sure he was thinking, 'Someone's pulling that line away from me. It's those Leinster fans, breathing in and sucking the dust back off the line.' But he finally made it and he didn't come up

off the ball for ages. Afterwards a lot of people said, 'Was it emotion that made him stay down? Or was it exhaustion?' Exhaustion. Fair play to him.

RONAN O'GARA: Trevor had been class in the quarter-final and he was class in the semi-final. In the big, big games – where he needed to stand up – he gave the whole team a new dimension. He didn't start well and he'll admit that himself, but it's a sign of a good player when he can raise his game for the big occasion. Our Celtic League team is different to our European Cup team. Maybe that's not what the squad want to hear

> **TREVOR HAD BEEN CLASS IN THE QUARTER-FINAL AND HE WAS CLASS IN THE SEMI-FINAL. IN THE BIG, BIG GAMES — WHERE HE NEEDED TO STAND UP — HE GAVE THE WHOLE TEAM A NEW DIMENSION.**

or what the management want to hear, but that's reality in my eyes. You've got bigger characters in the European Cup and you've better players. I think I know how to get the best out of Trevor. He needs to be geed up and he needs to be challenged – not just by the opposition but by his own players.

DONNCHA O'CALLAGHAN: Even at the end, we were telling each other, 'Just keep playing, keep playing!' It was like we had a fear that they could score thirty points in no time, that they could still do it. We had too much respect for them to let up. We just kept going at them and for me anyway that's the greatest compliment you could pay any team – respecting them so much that you go at them full-on for every second.

PAUL O'CONNELL: We'd played three weeks in a row together. and match fitness was through the roof. That's how we put in such a great eighty-minute performance, something we hadn't really done all year. You can put it down to how much we wanted it and all that, but you can't ignore the fact that we'd had proper time together as a squad.

MARCUS HORAN: Freddie was superb that day. It was the worst eighty minutes I've ever put down, sitting in the stand watching that. You just have no control. I only relaxed when Rog scored – and you still have that bit of anxiety. You're high as a kite on the final whistle. And then thirty minutes after it you just hit a low and you realize, 'God, I wasn't involved.' And I still have to get fit.

FEDERICO PUCCIARIELLO: It was one of the great games in my whole career. I was so disappointed with that yellow card, but when Felipe missed the kick from the penalty,

Opposite top: **O'Gara embraces Brian O'Driscoll after the final whistle**
Opposite bottom: **In from the cold: Rob Henderson and Anthony Horgan, both of whom returned to the side against Leinster**

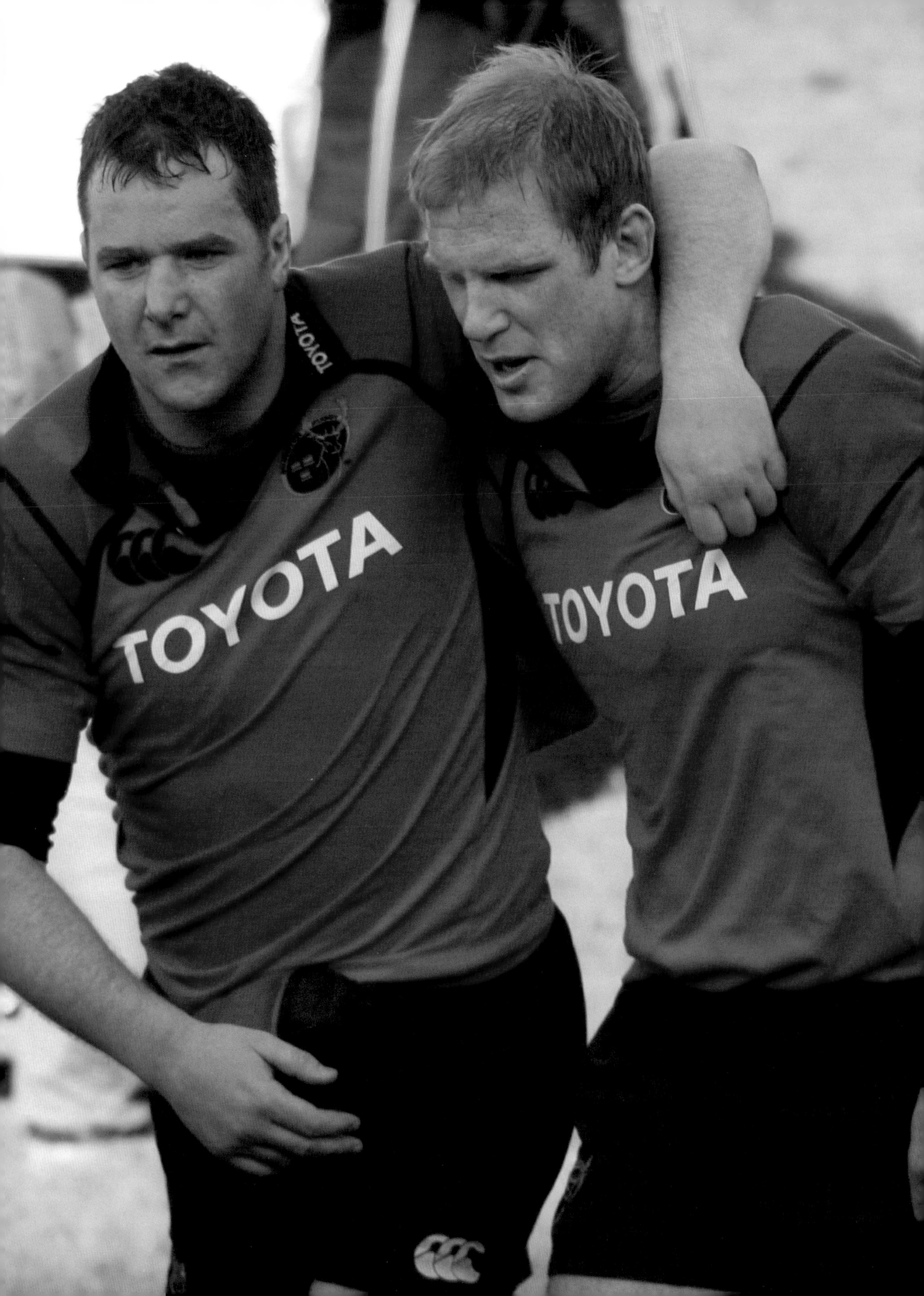
TOYOTA
TOYOTA
TOYOTA

I say, 'That's a good sign.' I would have broken the bench if he had scored. Two policemen were telling me to calm down. I said, 'Calm? I can't be calm. I am so sorry, but I can't do anything else.' When Ronan scored the try, I was jumping around and screaming I was so happy. The pressure on that game, it was too much.

RONAN O'GARA, POST-MATCH TV INTERVIEW: See I'm a proud Cork man, and Paulie here is a proud Limerick man, and we have to walk the streets amongst our people tomorrow.

SHAUN PAYNE: Leinster did us three favours. They beat Bath. They beat Toulouse. And they lost to us.

When the team got off the train at Limerick late that night, they made for Jerry Flannery's pub in Catherine Street. Thanks to Paul O'Connell, half the country was made aware that it had reopened its doors for business that weekend. Looking surprisingly well, the proprietor and his plugger-in-chief sat at the bar the following morning and reflected on events at Lansdowne Road while the evening news camera rolled.

For Biarritz Olympique, who they would face at the Millennium Stadium in Cardiff, there was deep respect. O'Connell rubbished the theory, fast gaining ground, that at the third time of asking Munster's final triumph was somehow written in the stars. 'It's no one's destiny to win it, it's the best team on the day,' he said. 'There's no destiny in this.'

The final was just under four weeks away, giving Marcus Horan hope of being fit to withstand the might of the Biarritz tighthead Census Johnson, and allowing John Kelly and Rob Henderson recovery time for their shoulder and ankle injuries. Christian Cullen was also fighting hard to be ready and for Alan Quinlan, so badly injured in the opening match of the European campaign, there was also a chance. For Frankie Sheahan, injured in the same match as Quinlan, the outlook was bleak. He was fighting a losing battle against time.

Others would cause serious concern in the run-up to the big day, with O'Connell injuring his ankle in a Celtic League match at the Ospreys two weeks before it and

O'Gara going down with food poisoning in the week of the match. All of these, with the exception of Sheahan and the luckless Cullen – who came back from his shoulder injury but then hurt an ankle – would eventually pull through.

SHAUN PAYNE: We moved on quickly and started thinking about the final. We analysed everything about Biarritz. Up and down and back to front. Absolutely everything.

GEORGE MURRAY, VIDEO ANALYST: We plan ahead, prepare for all eventualities. Whether it was Biarritz or Bath who won the other semi-final, we had already started gathering the footage. What we're looking for is something frequent, an area to attack. The one thing about Biarritz that was overwhelming throughout all the games we looked at was that no team went out and attacked them, played the game flat on the gain line against them, got in their face. A lot of teams got into a kicking duel with them – and they lost. Sale stood off them and let them get a lead – then it was hard to get back into the game. We felt there was an opportunity to play right through the middle of them.

ANTHONY FOLEY: They had Traille, Yachvili and Brusque, who all can kick the ball from a mile out, so it was going to be important that when we had the ball we didn't give it away too cheaply and end up inside our own half defending the whole time. We rarely saw Sale attacking inside their twenty-two. We felt that, if we remained patient and made them defend for long periods, we would get points.

DECLAN KIDNEY: Twelve days before the final, on the Monday morning after we played the Ospreys in Wales, five of us sat down to come up with a game plan. There was myself, Jim Williams, Brian Hickey, Tony McGahan and Steady [Graham Steadman]. The original think-tank. Some ideas were thrown out, others were adjusted. Most good meetings last less than an hour, but four hours later we came away with pages full of ideas. The trick then is to condense that into fifteen minutes for the players. You can't give them too much information, because if they go out thinking about the opposition too much they forget to play themselves. You take it to a few of the senior players and say, 'This is what we're thinking of doing.' Sometimes they're for it, sometimes

> **THE ONE THING ABOUT BIARRITZ THAT WAS OVERWHELMING THROUGHOUT ALL THE GAMES WE LOOKED AT WAS THAT NO TEAM WENT OUT AND ATTACKED THEM, PLAYED THE GAME FLAT ON THE GAIN LINE AGAINST THEM, GOT IN THEIR FACE.**

not. You talk it through and then you go with a plan to the whole team. You say, 'What do ye all think?' Because at the end of the day, they're the ones who have to be comfortable with it. The easiest thing in the world is to come up with an idea. They have to execute it.

We felt the first twenty minutes were going to be vital, because they were inclined to put teams away in that period. When you get to that stage of a competition you can't expect to find glaring weaknesses. We picked up a few things. They were leaving their short side a bit exposed and crowding the middle of the pitch. They play a big pressure game; I suppose we do, too. We wouldn't have been true to ourselves if we'd tried to change our game at that stage. If something was good enough to get you to a final, why reinvent the wheel? If they were going to be better than us at what we both do well, they were going to win.

ANTHONY FOLEY: We were both going to have a right good crack at one another. I knew the hits would be going in everywhere.

PETER STRINGER: All the way up to the final we had supporters coming up to us saying, 'This is our year – I can really feel it. We're going to do it this time!' But that has always been the case. I've been hearing it every year since 2000. All you can say is, 'Ah shur, we'll keep chipping away at it and hopefully it'll go our way.' You're setting yourself up for a fall if you say anything else. You feel conscious that you're repeating yourself all the time, coming out with the same lines, but the thing is to keep a smile on your face when you're saying it, to make light of it. If you get too serious with everyone you know you're into a big discussion.

DECLAN KIDNEY: I don't think anybody is beyond listening to advice from the people who support us. Sometimes you act on it, sometimes you just hear it.

ANTHONY FOLEY: There was a lot of talk about destiny, and you do look at little things that happened throughout the year, the bonus points we got at crucial stages. For a minute you wonder if it might be your year. Then you remember that we'd been there before – the Miracle Match [against Gloucester], beating Toulouse in Bordeaux – and there was no destiny then. So you just focus in on the game.

PETER STRINGER: There was a lot of talk about their scrum-half, Yachvili, but I always hear that. He's a talented guy, but I prefer being the underdog. I like the challenge of that, the chance to go out and prove people wrong.

DECLAN KIDNEY: You try to learn from other years. There was nothing I could do to prepare them for that last mile leading to the ground. But I thought I could prepare them for what they were going to experience when they walked out for the kick-off.

On the Tuesday before the final, the players reported for training at Musgrave Park and noticed some speakers near the pitch. They were Kidney's doing: he was about to become the DJ from hell. His idea was to give the players a sense of what the noise levels in Cardiff would be like. On his instructions, five tracks lasting twenty-three minutes were cut together, with crowd noise laid down on top. When Kidney was asked what kind of music he wanted, he replied: 'I don't care – as long as it's loud.'

At first, the players were merely bewildered. The first track was a live version of U2's 'Where The Streets Have No Name', but when that gave way to the deafening 'Thunderstruck' by AC/DC and 'Welcome To The Jungle' by Guns 'n' Roses, both the players and the speakers were reaching the point of explosion.

DONNCHA O'CALLAGHAN: I felt like knocking his head off. It just annoyed me. I was saying, 'There's absolutely no reason for this.' We'd just played Leinster, and the noise there was massive, so I just couldn't see the point of it. The racket was unbelievable.

ROB HENDERSON: Oh my God! One of them went, '*Thun*-der! Na na na *na* na!' I just couldn't get that out of my head. It was like standing next to those deafening music systems they used to carry round in the eighties for a bit of breakdancing. That's how loud it was. This was supposed to be getting us ready for the final. Oh, that sounds like it! I feel like I'm in Cardiff now. It's exactly the same!

I don't know where the music came from, but the idea of Deccie listening to this stuff on the way to training was horrific. Declan, you've got no hair! You're not a long-haired lover, love. You're not a rocker. Let it go.

DECLAN KIDNEY: They were going mental. On the Friday, Hendo said, 'By the way, that music you played was crap.' I said I would pass on his comments. It wasn't meant to be good. I could have told him, 'What were you doing listening to it? You were supposed to be concentrating on what you were doing.'

RONAN O'GARA: I've had Deccie as a coach for fifteen years and he's been great, a huge influence on my career. In the build-up to the final he was cranky enough. I think he was probably as nervous as anyone. There was just so much at stake, you wouldn't be human if you didn't feel it. I was feeling terrible all that week and I couldn't train for most of it, because of the food poisoning. But I wasn't the only one struggling. Different people had their own battles to get themselves right.

TREVOR HALSTEAD: I started getting a lot of text messages from the guys back home. The nerves were building and by Thursday they were full-on. The lads had been there before and lost, but I had my own pressure – I'd lost my own finals. I had lost Currie Cup finals back home and the Super 12 final in 2001. I was thinking, 'I can't lose another one. I just can't.'

MARCUS HORAN: When we got to the week of the match I just said, 'Right, I have to go balls-out here and if this calf goes, it goes.' The lads were great. They said, 'There's no point in tip-toeing around this, you just have to go hard at it.' I did, and the confidence grew. Some guys had sleepless nights that week, but I was totally focused getting my calf right so I slept fine.

ALAN QUINLAN: I was holding out a small bit of hope. It's hard to come in every day for six months on your own, hard to keep motivated. There were days when I didn't think I could get back, but Kirsty Peacock, Fergal O'Callaghan, Sean Whitney and the Ireland rehab specialist Brian Green were so helpful to me when I was down and out. I hung on to that glimmer of hope.

Late in the week, Declan named me in the twenty-two and I can't tell you how much it meant to me. But it was difficult, too. I took Stephen Keogh's place in the match twenty-two and I felt bad for him. Frankie Sheahan, too – he got injured the same day as me. I was the lucky one, and my heart went out to those two guys and all the other guys who weren't lucky enough to be in the squad for the final. Everyone had worked their socks off all year.

DECLAN KIDNEY: To say it was tough telling Stephen Keogh he wasn't in the twenty-two would be a great understatement. But if it's that tough to tell him, how hard is it to hear it? It was a real last-minute decision because we didn't know who was going to be fit. I told him on the Thursday and he said he'd had an inkling. If you're a player, you're always suspicious if you're not named in the thing straight up. To do that to a person, when they have bust their chops to be where they are – to take it from them is just so hugely disappointing for them. I told him and then gave him space to adjust to it before the team was announced to the squad.

AFX WIRE STORY, 19 MAY 2006, 16:36: CARDIFF – Biarritz captain Thomas Lièvremont has returned from injury to lead the French champions in Saturday's European Cup rugby union final here at the Millennium Stadium. Meanwhile, prop Marcus Horan is back in the Munster 1st XV. Munster, twice losing finalists and yet to win European club rugby union's biggest prize, may be the sentimental favourites but captain Anthony Foley said: 'We have no divine right to win it. We have a fifty-fifty chance, and we will give it our best shot.' With a bad weather forecast, Lièvremont was keen that the Millennium Stadium's retractable roof be closed come the kick-off.

Biarritz: Nicolas Brusque; Jean-Baptiste Gobelet, Philippe Bidabe, Damien Traille, Sereli Bobo; Julien Peyrelongue, Dimitri Yachvili; Thomas Lièvremont (capt), Imanol Harinordoquy, Serge Betsen; David Couzinet, Jérôme Thion; Census Johnson, Benoît August, Petru Vladimir Balan. Replacements: Benjamin Noirot, Benoît Lecouls, Olivier Olibeau, Thierry Dusautoir, Manuel Carizza, Julien Dupuy, Federico Martin-Arramburu.

Munster: Shaun Payne; Anthony Horgan, John Kelly, Trevor Halstead, Ian Dowling; Ronan O'Gara, Peter Stringer; Anthony Foley (capt), David Wallace, Denis Leamy; Paul O'Connell, Donncha O'Callaghan; John Hayes, Jerry Flannery, Marcus Horan. Replacements: Denis Fogarty, Federico Pucciariello, Mick O'Driscoll, Alan Quinlan, Tomas O'Leary, Jeremy Manning, Rob Henderson.

DECLAN KIDNEY: We flew over on the Friday. For the 2002 final we arrived a day earlier but this time we wanted them to be in their own environment for as long as possible before the match. It was all about conserving energy. We knew exactly how long it would take to get from the airport to the ground and then back to the hotel. We researched the timings. Nothing was left to chance.

DONNCHA O'CALLAGHAN: Normally I prefer to go two days before, so that I can rest up. I was cursing the fact that we were going on the Friday, but in the end I was glad. It meant I had less time to think about the final, less time to worry. I couldn't have taken two days of table tennis outside my room either.

CHAPTER 14
DONNCHA O'CALLAGHAN'S STORY

❝ THE RESPECT OF THE PLAYERS AROUND ME IS WHAT I'M AFTER. ❞

I was born on my brother Ultan's eighth birthday in March 1979. My father took him to the maternity hospital and said, 'Look what we got you for your birthday!' He thought he was getting a Subbuteo game so he wasn't very impressed, but ever since that day he has looked out for me.

My dad died when I was six. I remember a lot about him, mostly his passion for sport. He was a mad Liverpool fan and he used to bring us down to Flower Lodge to watch Cork City play, and any bit of sport that was going on, he got us involved in it. When something like that happens, families pull together, and that has been the case for us. My best friends are my family. I've three brothers and one sister. My oldest brother, Eddie, took on a lot of responsibility; he became a father figure in our house.

One of the reasons the Munster team means so much to me is because the parents of the players have a great bond. The O'Garas, the Horgans, the O'Driscolls, the Horans – all of them – have become great friends. They pull my mum in and they look out for her, and that matters an awful lot to me. It's a very family-orientated squad. You'd come in after the match and you'd get the same greeting off Mary Quinlan, Alan's mum, as you would off your own mother. Guys like Shaun Payne join us, and their families become part of it too. People make a big effort to welcome them.

The first day I walked into Bishopstown Community School, there was a teacher called Pat McDonnell who was looking for boys interested in playing hurling. I put up my hand.

'Are you an O'Callaghan?' he said.

ONE OF THE REASONS THE MUNSTER TEAM MEANS SO MUCH TO ME IS BECAUSE THE PARENTS OF THE PLAYERS HAVE A GREAT BOND. THE O'GARAS, THE HORGANS, THE O'DRISCOLLS, THE HORANS — ALL OF THEM — HAVE BECOME GREAT FRIENDS. THEY PULL MY MUM IN AND THEY LOOK OUT FOR HER, AND THAT MATTERS AN AWFUL LOT TO ME.

'Yes.'

'You're not allowed to hurl.'

I think he was afraid to give the O'Callaghan boys a hurley. I was probably made for rugby and nothing else. I knew from an early age that it was the game for me. That, and the fact that I was fairly useless at football, which was the big sport in Bishopstown.

I used to go and watch Ultan and I'd be saying, 'That's my brother there.' Being at those matches really gave me a hunger for it. My brothers would kick the shit out of me in the front garden, but I think I learned more there than watching any amount of rugby.

I'm a professional player, but even if I didn't get a penny I'd still want to play for Munster. Every time I come into the dressing room after wearing the jersey, I can't wait for the next time. I never take it for granted – maybe it's because I had to wait so long to get it in the first place. I worked hard to get the Number 4 jersey off Gaillimh, and these fellows are going to have to work harder to get it off me. I arrived on the Munster scene when I was nineteen, and it felt like a very long apprenticeship before I finally broke through, but I'm glad I went through that because I feel like I've earned it. If it had come too easy, maybe I wouldn't have the same drive and desire that I do now.

When I started making the team, I got a bit of a reputation for messing and joking all over the place. Every time I'd chat to someone in the paper or on radio, they would

say, 'Tell us about your latest prank.' If you talk to the people who know me, they'll tell you that I might mess around a bit but when I get on the pitch I'm very serious. I was glad to get rid of that tag. I wouldn't like anyone to think I'm a messer. My rugby means a huge amount to me.

The respect of the players around me is what I'm after. The only thing I worry about is not performing for them. Me and Marcus, we broke through together, and I'm behind him in the scrum. I will give every ounce of energy I have to help him. I'd never want him to turn around and say, 'You let me down there.' When we're in that scrum, I want to put my shoulder through his ass, because every time he gives me a lift in the lineout he wants it to be the best lift he can give. Helping him is a huge thing for me, and that was something that was on my mind coming up to the final, because I knew how gutted he was to miss out on the Leinster match.

The Sunday after we beat Leinster, I went into Supervalu in Glanmire and I'd say it was the closest I'll ever get to being David Beckham or a Cork hurler or something. They had me signing autographs and standing for camera phones. There was this Polish girl serving me and she was looking around wondering who the hell I was. But that match, I think, created an interest in rugby that was never there before in Cork. Everyone watched it, and you knew they were all going to be watching the final as well.

This might sound a bit weird, but I actually prefer playing against French teams. I tend to do well against them. We had huge respect for Biarritz. They had got to the final without playing their best rugby, and it was obvious that on their day they could give any team a hiding. We knew it was going to be hugely physical, that we were going to have to take a lot of punishment.

CHAPTER 15

MAKE IT HAPPEN

> **I FIRMLY BELIEVE THAT ANY MAN'S FINEST HOUR, HIS GREATEST FULFILMENT OF ALL HE HOLDS DEAR, IS THE MOMENT WHEN HE HAS WORKED HIS HEART OUT IN A GOOD CAUSE AND LIES EXHAUSTED ON THE FIELD OF BATTLE – VICTORIOUS.' – VINCE LOMBARDI, QUOTED IN A BOOKLET GIVEN TO EACH OF THE PLAYERS BY MUNSTER SUPPORTERS ON THE EVE OF THE FINAL**

Of the 74,534 spectators in the Millennium Stadium that Saturday afternoon, it was estimated that 65,000 were supporting Munster. At 2.58 p.m., the teams appeared in the tunnel, led out by Anthony Foley and Thomas Lièvremont. The Frenchman stared at the ground in front of him, Foley looked dead straight ahead. As the players emerged, the U2 song 'Vertigo' was drowned out by a roar that rose up and hit the closed stadium roof and then reverberated around the ground. Donncha O'Callaghan was toward the back of the line and when he heard the noise, it crossed his mind that Declan Kidney should have brought bigger speakers to the training session.

Marcus Horan was behind Foley, then came Ian Dowling, who zigzagged across the pitch with the exuberance of youth. Behind him, Peter Stringer ran to his right and then stole a glance over his shoulder at the East Stand. Paul O'Connell was one of the last players out. As he reached the pitch he bent down to touch it. Then he blessed himself.

PETER STRINGER: You prepare yourself for what you think it might be like running out and then you experience something far beyond that. It sent shivers all over my body.

The noise was pulsing with me as I was running. It might sound strange, but I could nearly hear the steps I was taking. It wasn't a constant sound I could hear as I was running. It hit your ears in waves. I had to look around, just to see what it was like in the stands.

PAUL O'CONNELL: My dad always told me there were three things I had to do before every match – bless myself going out on to the pitch, wear a gumshield and keep my discipline. When we ran out for the final in 2002 the noise was massive – I remember looking across at Gaillimh and not being able to hear him. This time the noise was deafening, but I had my wits about me. When we went into the huddle I was saying something, and it was obvious that everyone could hear me. There's no way the noise was less than it was in 2002 so maybe we were overawed back then. Maybe we were listening to the noise.

I had tweaked my neck that morning in training and I'd got a lot of massage on it. Went out for the warm-up, and the pain got worse. I was getting worried about the first scrum, thinking my neck could go, so I went over to the doc and he gave me an anti-inflammatory injection a few minutes before kick-off.

DECLAN KIDNEY: I was sitting in the stand. Front row, middle tier, great view. Jim Williams was pitchside, and the rest of the coaching staff were alongside me. Everyone was miked up. I wanted them to give me whatever they thought, but I said, 'Don't give me so much that I can't handle it.' Watching it is tough for any coach. I suppose I do eat up inside. They put a monitor on a Premiership soccer coach once and his heart rate went through the roof. I don't think my reading would be far off that.

DONNCHA O'CALLAGHAN: They kicked off, and I thought, 'Bloody hell – here we go. This is it.'

SHAUN PAYNE: The plan would normally be for me to run on to the ball and take it, but because it was so loud David [Wallace] didn't hear me call for the ball. He was under it, he went for it too and we ran into each other. Straight away the ball is turned over to them.

> # ❝ MY DAD ALWAYS TOLD ME THERE WERE THREE THINGS I HAD TO DO BEFORE EVERY MATCH – BLESS MYSELF GOING OUT ON TO THE PITCH, WEAR A GUMSHIELD AND KEEP MY DISCIPLINE. ❞

RONAN O'GARA: Two minutes into it, they were coming at us, but it didn't look like there was much danger. I was outside John Kelly, and he told me to wedge, to push out. I was expecting Bidabe to pass it to Brusque but he got a fend on John, pushed him off. Of all the guys you wouldn't expect that to happen to, John would be right up there.

JOHN KELLY: It was a good fend, but I was gutted that I let him past me. I hadn't played for four weeks, not since going off against Leinster, and that rustiness cost me. Bidabe went through the gap I'd left, gave it to Bobo, and all of a sudden we were in trouble.

ANTHONY FOLEY: I saw Bobo trying to keep his feet in – he was tip-toeing down the sideline. I saw [Dave] Pearson [touch judge] having a good look, and as I got there he was saying, 'No that's a good try, no question there.' We were standing there waiting for the conversion and they showed it on the big screen. When our fans saw his foot go in touch there were boos all around the place.

DECLAN KIDNEY: My reaction? The first word was probably four letters.

PAUL O'CONNELL: We all have one of those a season, but if you're good enough then you make up for it. We had a huddle, and Rags put his hand up and said, 'Look, I missed a tackle – it won't happen again.' We figured out what went wrong and we put it behind us. Job done, move on.

ANTHONY FOLEY: You can get caught up in that. You can think, 'Here it comes – another hard-luck story,' because we've had plenty of them. But in fairness to the lads we went

straight back up there and we got a three-pointer, something on the board. That was crucial. Then we just cut loose and went after them. We started playing our own game.

JOHN HAYES: I had played against [Petru] Balan once before, in the quarter-final last year. He's a hugely powerful man. He likes to set up mauls off the side of rucks. I watched him in a lot of videos, but the first scrum in the game will teach you a lot more than any video. I knew he'd want to make a big impression early on, so I had to get stuck into him early.

MARCUS HORAN: The first scrum was in their half, and it was their put-in. I hadn't thought about [Census] Johnson too much beforehand, but I knew he was a big unit. I felt the first hit would be all-important. I was worried about how my calf would stand up to the first scrum. We engaged and I hit as hard as I could going in. I remember saying to myself, 'Fuck it, this is good!' At the second scrum I tried to put extra weight on the bad leg, just to really test it. After that I was like, 'Right – you're in now. Keep it going.'

SHAUN PAYNE: About five minutes after their try, Brusque kicked it down towards touch on my left. I ran over and caught it but there was a lot of momentum there and I was tip-toeing near the line. I thought I'd managed to stay in, but the flag went up. I was well upset about that. The first thing that came into my mind was, 'Jesus, Bobo just stepped out for the try, and here they're calling me, and I haven't stepped on the line.' I've gone back and looked at it and half a centimetre of my toe was on the line, but at the time I was well upset. I expect to get my field position right in our twenty-two. Two mistakes inside the first ten minutes is not acceptable.

ANTHONY FOLEY: We were really getting into the game when we got a penalty in their half, kickable range. I looked at Rog, and Rog looked at me. He said, 'Corner?' and I said, 'Yeah – let's go for it.' At times you have a team by the throat, and they give away a penalty to relieve pressure. They think, 'OK, we'll concede three rather than seven.' You get your three points, you jog back to the halfway line, and then they kick off and they're attacking you.

Opposite: Paul O'Connell snags a high lineout throw; later, Munster would prosper with a new lineout formation, aiming at Donncha O'Callaghan at the front

Trevor Halstead, who scored Munster's first try, fends off Serge Betsen

It was early in the game, and I thought, 'We've got to make a statement here and show them our intent. We're going after this, we're leaving nothing behind us today.' We went for it, kicked to the corner and it didn't come off. Then we went over to the other side of the pitch and got another penalty. Went for it again and that didn't come off, but our intent had been shown. Everybody on the pitch knew what we were trying to do. We were saying to them, 'You can give away penalties but that's not going to stop us going at you.'

RONAN O'GARA: I agreed completely. In the other finals we probably would have kicked them, but it showed the boldness about us. We had more belief in our ability to score tries. You just get a feel for a game that you're playing in. Even at that stage of the match, it was obvious there was something about the team that wasn't there in previous years. We were far more stable. We realized that we had to play and express ourselves. I felt there was a try coming.

TREVOR HALSTEAD: It was a great period of play for us, constant pressure. We were attacking them, and the move had gone through quite a few phases. We'd taken them all the way up the right-hand side of the field. Denis Leamy came short off me, and we had an overlap on them.

DENIS LEAMY: No matter how good a defence is, if you run hard you eventually bust them.

PETER STRINGER: The forwards had done really well – they picked and went and drove it in close, sucked a lot of Biarritz guys in. We were getting closer, and it was time for the backs to have a crack at it. I got the ball away to Rog, and he had Trevor outside him and two more outside Trevor.

Anthony Horgan unloads as he takes a hit

> ❝ HE HAD THE BALL UNDER HIS ARM AND TWO REALLY BIG
> GUYS TO GET PAST. GOBELET, THEIR RIGHT WINGER, MADE
> A TACKLE ON HIM AND HE'S A MASSIVE GUY, HUGE. BUT
> TREVOR TOOK THEM HEAD-ON. HE JUST BASHED THE TWO
> OF THEM OUT OF THE WAY. ❞

RONAN O'GARA: We had four on two, but I nearly messed it up. I expected Trevor to be a little deeper because I couldn't hear him, so I took a fair bit out of it. I was a good catch by him – and it was a big call to go for the line because he had men outside him.

TREVOR HALSTEAD: I just knew if Rog gave it to me early it was on for me. I took the ball flat and at that stage I knew I wasn't going to pass because there was a gap. It wasn't a big gap and it actually closed out on me, but there was no way I wasn't going to score that close to the line. I had the outside centre and the winger in front of me and I just went in for the crash. There wasn't that much thought in it. It was just, 'I am going straight over these guys and I am going to score. No matter what.'

PETER STRINGER: He had the ball under his arm and two really big guys to get past. Gobelet, their right winger, made a tackle on him and he's a massive guy, huge. But Trevor took them head-on. He just bashed the two of them out of the way.

TREVOR HALSTEAD: I rolled out of the tackle and put the ball down. At that moment I thought, 'Is it real? Have I scored? Have I done it?' I looked up and the guys were standing in front of me going mad, and the crowd had gone absolutely berserk. For a while I was still in a daze. Then there was another feeling – we're back in the game. Now we start. I remember walking back with my hands on my head. It was so *loud*.

TIM GLOVER, *INDEPENDENT ON SUNDAY*: There were twice as many red jerseys here than there are when Wales are playing a Test. It is as well the roof was closed because more of

Opposite: Ronan O'Gara nails one of his several excellent
kicks in the final, with Jim Williams looking on

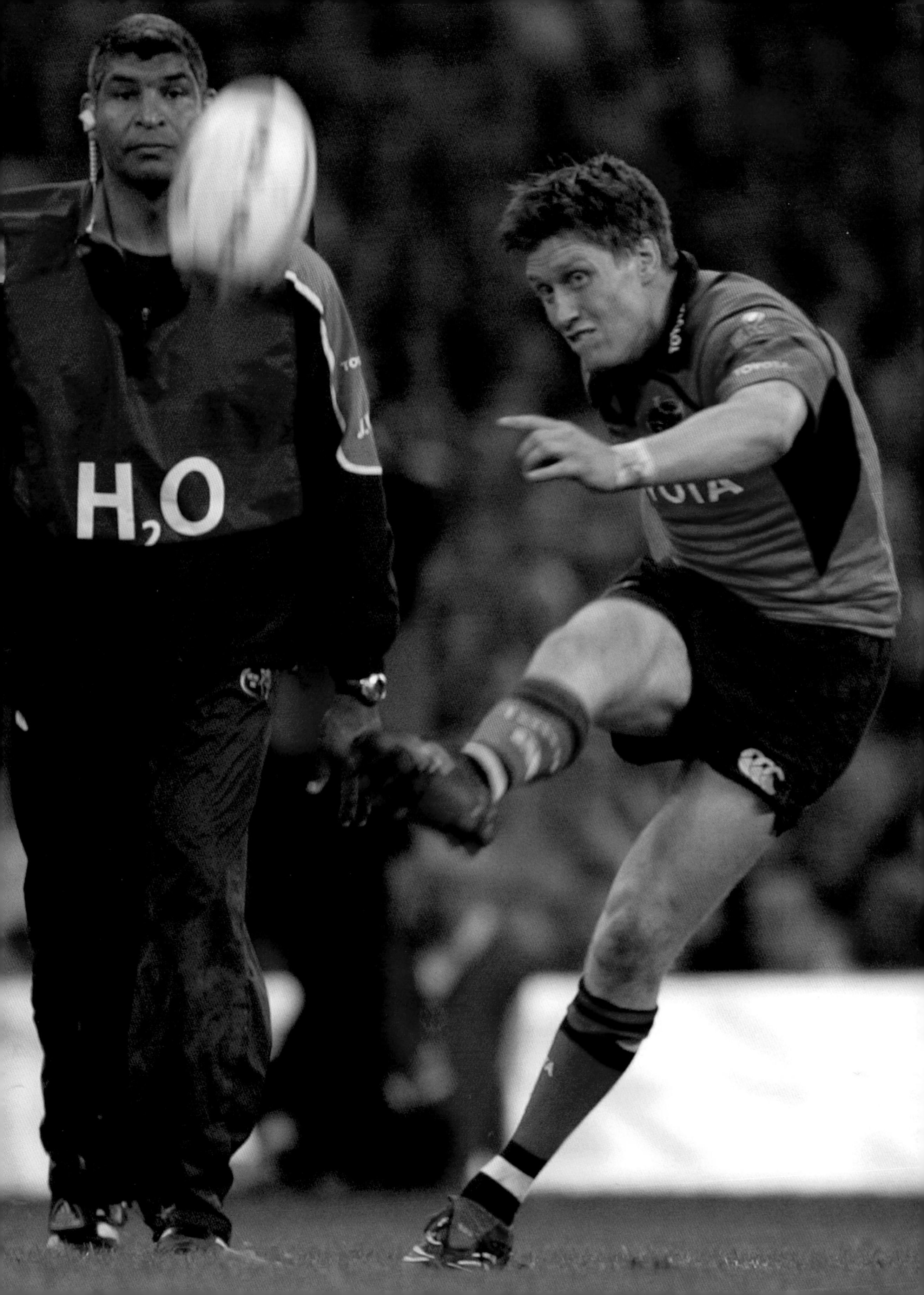
H_2O

them would have probably arrived by abseil, parachute and hot air balloon. Biarritz knew what to expect but they were still engulfed.

MARCUS HORAN: There were a lot of pick-and-gos before that try. We took the ball up the guts and they were out on their feet – they were shattered. After we'd run back, Jerry Flannery roared over me on the halfway line: 'They're fucked, they're fucked! Let's sow it into 'em!'

RONAN O'GARA: The pace was frenetic, and I was blowing hard. It was a hell of a lot faster than the Leinster game. The heart rate was going mad. I stood over the conversion and I felt I wasn't going to miss. I felt like I was in the groove, bullet-proof. I was saying to myself in the build-up, 'It's one thing Munster winning but you've got to do yourself justice on a personal level too.' The way I saw it, if I went out there and had a good game, then we were going to win.

I struck it well and made it a seven-pointer. That try was a reward for the positive attitude we'd showed. They got it back to 10-all not long after, but we kept coming at them and they gave away another penalty.

GEORGE HOOK, RTE TV ANALYST: Well, the extraordinary thing here, I think, is that Munster are displaying a strange attitude towards kicking goals. They turned down a certain six points earlier on. It's all very well to say they're 10-all now, but I think they need to take the points.

PAUL O'CONNELL: You make a decision and you go with it. Whether it's right or wrong, if fifteen guys go for it then normally it comes out the right way in the end.

RYLE NUGENT, RTE COMMENTATOR: Here comes the decision now. And it is … well, it's to go down the line again. It's brave but the question is – at the end of eighty [minutes] will it prove to have been foolhardy?

ANTHONY FOLEY: People who question those decisions will never be in that situation themselves. At times I've spoken to Deccie about this, and he doesn't want to discuss it.

Ronan O'Gara and Donncha O'Callaghan look excited as David Wallace moves into a gap

He just says, 'You're the guy out on the pitch, it's your decision.' He doesn't want to interfere with our instincts. And our instincts were telling us to go and win the game, to keep driving at them. We went for the lineout, took it on a few phases and then we got a scrum, close enough to their line, over on the right.

PETER STRINGER: I felt this was a part of the pitch where a scrum-half could make a difference. I'd been looking at their scrums on my video iPod and writing down things I might be able to exploit. A couple of times, when the scrum wheeled, their winger moved across and left a gap. But every scrum is different, and you never know how it's going to turn out.

As I was bending down to put the ball into the scrum, I saw that Bobo had moved off his wing and stepped inside. Our winger [Anthony Horgan] had gone infield, and Bobo had nobody to mark. So straight away I was thinking, 'There's an opportunity

O'Connell on the rampage

here.' Just before I put the ball in, I had a quick glance at where Bobo was standing. I was conscious that I didn't want him to guess what I was thinking, so I just looked for a split-second and I never looked at him again after that. There was a backline move called, and obviously they were expecting to get the ball. In a position like that, a good attacking position, Rog would automatically assume he's getting it. But if it was going to work I had to sell it to my own team-mates as well as the opposition.

RONAN O'GARA: I was either going to hit Hoggy or else throw it across to Trevor. I mean, 999 times out of a thousand I'm going to get that ball as soon as it comes out of the scrum.

JERRY FLANNERY: There was a lot of shit in the papers. You know, Biarritz have such a strong scrum and they're going to dick Munster. OK, there were one or two scrummages at the start that put us under pressure. But I just thought, 'Let's see how tired these fellas get as the game goes on. Wait and see how they're doing against us then. Don't judge us on the first two, judge us on the whole game.' Hayes and Marcus were doing huge work all around the field. Then we hit that scrum really solid and I can remember feeling our surge get stronger and getting the little nudge on. It opened up that split second that Stringer needed.

PETER STRINGER: It was a perfect scrum. It didn't move much, but I didn't need much. Betsen was on the blindside, facing me, and it forced him step a bit to his right. That meant he had more ground to cover if he was going to get me. And because it was such a solid scrum from us, he had to stay down and drive into it.

I shaped to pass and then at the last second I spun around. After that first glance I hadn't looked again to see where Bobo was. That was a gamble, but it was the key to it. I couldn't afford the risk of making eye contact with him, or even glancing up the blindside, because if he'd seen that he could have read my mind. I didn't know where he was when I made the break. For all I knew he could have come back over – he could have been standing there in front of me.

I knew Betsen was on the side of the scrum, but I couldn't see him either because I had my back to him. I knew the line I was going to take. I wasn't just going to pick and run straight – I was going to dart around to make sure I got outside him. I took off and there was no sign of Bobo. Once Betsen realized what was happening I was gone past him. I ran over the goal-line and I ran another three metres. Bobo came back and stopped me going further infield. I had to get the ball down and for the first time in my life I dived. I don't why then and never before. Something just came over me.

" WE HIT THAT SCRUM REALLY SOLID AND I CAN REMEMBER FEELING OUR SURGE GET STRONGER AND GETTING THE LITTLE NUDGE ON. IT OPENED UP THAT SPLIT SECOND THAT STRINGER NEEDED. "

" I TOOK OFF AND THERE WAS NO SIGN OF BOBO. ONCE BETSEN REALIZED WHAT WAS HAPPENING I WAS GONE PAST HIM. "

I wrapped my right arm around the ball so that it was tight to my chest and I dived. I was holding on to it so tightly – there was no way I was going to drop it.

MARCUS HORAN: Sometimes when you're down there you hear a muffled roar and you're hoping it's going to be a penalty for us. The cheer we heard was too loud to be anything good for Biarritz. Then we stood up out of it, and the place was going mad. When you work that hard, it's great to realize that you only have to jog back to the halfway line and not hit a ruck. We were delighted that Strings did that for us, you know?

JOHN HAYES: I came up out of the scrum and said to Leamy, 'What the fuck happened there?' I couldn't believe it was that easy. Their tight five were the same. You could see them thinking, 'Where are we going now?' Next thing they realized a try had been scored. I didn't have a clue how he'd scored until I saw it the following day.

PETER STRINGER: I couldn't let go. I couldn't jump around and milk it and do high fives or anything like that. I ran back and gave the ball to Rog for the conversion and he gave me a good solid hug. When some guys score they look for other guys to celebrate with, but I didn't make eye contact with anyone. I just wanted to get on with it. Rog kicked a really good conversion, and we were seven points up, but you can lose that lead in the blink of an eye.

JERRY FLANNERY: We kept going at them. Wally carried a ball into contact and I was running a line behind him. I thought he was going to go to deck, but he just kept driving his legs, taking their whole team back with him. Then Wally got up and said, 'Leg drive! Leg drive! We've got to keep working our leg drive!' There's a lot

'For the first time in my life I dived': Peter Stringer airborne before touching down his pivotal try at the end of the first half

of emotional stuff in the game – 'Come on lads, I'll die for you,' and all that. But I'd much rather hear a valid point that you can take on board quickly.

DAVID WALLACE: For a Number 7 it's about work rate at the breakdown. You're usually the first or second guy in there and if you're attacking you've got to make sure the ball comes back cleanly. Sometimes you've got to cross the line of what's legal, you've got to cheat to compete. I'm not endorsing violence or anything like that, but it's a case of being cute on the pitch, not getting caught. You research the referee. There are certain things in rugby you can get away with for a little bit – and you have to work out what those limits are. If you're slowing down the opposition's ball, one second at a breakdown can make a huge difference. So you slow it down for one or two seconds – but not three.

> # THEIR KICKING GAME WAS HURTING US WHEN WE WEREN'T PUTTING THE BALL OUT. THEY WERE GETTING HUGE RETURNS — BRUSQUE WAS HAMMERING US BACK INTO THE CORNERS, AND WE DIDN'T WANT TO BE PLAYING THE GAME THERE.

We believed that we were fitter than them – because Paulie kept telling us. Maybe it was true, maybe it wasn't – but we believed it, and if you keep telling yourself you're fitter then you keep trying harder and you keep giving it everything.

RONAN O'GARA: We went in at half-time and we were flying up the walls. It was an incredible pace. My face blew up, I was so hot. They were getting iced towels for me, and I was just trying to get myself composed again.

DECLAN KIDNEY: Their kicking game was hurting us when we weren't putting the ball out. They were getting huge returns – Brusque was hammering us back into the corners, and we didn't want to be playing the game there. The coaching staff went over a few things, but they'd given everything and they didn't need a lot of information from us. We always said we'd be an eighty-minute team, and they knew what was going to be required.

PETER STRINGER: We needed some quiet time to reflect and compose ourselves. When everyone starts talking it can be detrimental because there's too much being said, and nothing is going in. We didn't want to hear any big statements about being forty minutes away from the best experience of our careers. That wasn't going to do anyone any good. It had to be a lot simpler. Don't build it up to be anything more than what it is – forty minutes of rugby. We just had to keep on doing the basics, keep playing rugby, not get negative.

ANTHONY FOLEY: In a match like that, you don't get a second to say to yourself, 'I'm enjoying this.' Your thoughts are, 'What am I doing next? Where am I needed?' At this level you can't knock off for a second – look what happened to Bobo and Betsen. The information coming at us was short and sharp. The one thing I didn't like was the amount of talk about them. I said, 'Let's concentrate on ourselves here now, boys – we're talking about them too much.'

DONNCHA O'CALLAGHAN: We walked back out the tunnel thinking, 'Forty minutes, no regrets, give it everything, go and win it. Don't just sit back and expect it to happen. Make it happen.'

CHAPTER 16
THE WAIT IS OVER

❝ GET UP THEM STEPS AND GET THAT CUP. ❞

ROB HENDERSON: When you're a sub in a match like that, you always want to get on to the field – but first and foremost you want the side to win. There had been occasions during the season when I was on the bench thinking, 'Oh Jesus – will you ever put me on?' But that emotion wasn't there for the final. My feeling about it was, 'I am here to help support the team. If the team need me, I am ready. If they don't, then brilliant.' That is the absolute truth. Everyone had played a part in getting us there.

Along with the rest of the subs, I lined up at the tunnel before the second half started and clapped the lads on to the pitch. By doing that, you're giving them an extra gee-up, letting them know that you're there with them. What did I say?

'Axel – you're puffing.'

'Best of luck, Paulie. The hair's thinning a little bit.'

'Strings – you look great!'

'Trev – thanks for keeping me off the team.'

MARCUS HORAN: Jogging back out, I could feel my calf tightening. I knew then I was battling time to stay on. I just had to keep going for as long as I could.

ANTHONY FOLEY: We had a perfect start to the second half. Shaun Payne put up a garryowen and charged after it. Thion caught it, but we piled into him, and they ended up giving away a penalty.

RALPH KEYES, RTE TV CO-COMMENTATOR: And they won't be going to the corner on this one. You can be certain that Ronan O'Gara will now take the opportunity to try and stretch the lead immediately.

RONAN O'GARA: That was the one time I thought about it – because I knew how significant it was. I lost concentration for about ten seconds, so I had to just snap out of it and forget about the importance of the kick, forget about the scoreboard. I hit it well again and we were ten points in front, 20–10.

ANTHONY FOLEY: Straight after that penalty, John Hayes grabbed hold of Traille and he was wide open for a hit. I was first in line so I had a crack at him, and the boys came in behind me. He's a big player for them, and seeing him going backwards and turning over the ball was a boost for us. It's important that when you can inflict damage, you do it. I'm sure if one of our players was in that position he'd get opened as well. Then, for some reason, we started conceding ground. Our discipline slid a small bit, and we gave away a penalty. We knew going into the game that Yachvili kicks them from everywhere, so we paid for it.

DENIS LEAMY: Harinordoquy was having a brilliant match for them. Coming into it, I had a doubt or two about him. He came on the scene as a very young player and he was successful for a season or two, but then he went off the boil. I'm not saying he was overrated, but I've watched him a lot on television, watched him in the French league, and his body language was of a guy who wasn't interested. He was hanging out on the wing and he'd go down four or five times in a game. To be honest, I'd been more concerned about the other two back-row players, Betsen and Lièvremont. But Harinordoquy was outstanding – he's obviously a big-game player.

 THAT WAS THE ONE TIME I THOUGHT ABOUT IT – BECAUSE I KNEW HOW SIGNIFICANT IT WAS. I LOST CONCENTRATION FOR ABOUT TEN SECONDS, SO I HAD TO JUST SNAP OUT OF IT AND FORGET ABOUT THE IMPORTANCE OF THE KICK, FORGET ABOUT THE SCOREBOARD.

Opposite: 'Harinordoquy was having a brilliant match for them'
Overleaf and page 226: Dmitri Yachvili's work at scrum-half and with the boot kept Biarritz in the game to the end

After they got it back to 20–13 I came out of the defensive line and I knew Harinordoquy was going to step back in. I went to put a big shot on him. It was an easy enough tackle to make but he ducked his head a small bit and my arm went up and hit him on the neck. I knew straight away it was going to be a penalty and I was pissed off with myself. It was a sickening one to give away. Yachvili doesn't miss, not at all. He's a fantastic kicker. You're always hoping that he'll miss but I don't know that I've ever seen him do it. I knew what was coming.

KEITH WOOD: I was there with my wife and my youngest son. The atmosphere was unbelievable, but at that stage we were suffering. I find watching them difficult. Biarritz were coming back into it, and I was getting very frustrated and cranky. I starting saying, 'Jesus, come on! You're better than that. I know you are.'

ANTHONY FOLEY: We knew that a team with Biarritz's quality was going to have a purple patch and we're not arrogant enough to think that we can go through eighty minutes of rugby and be faultless. I felt we kicked the ball too much in the second half. We were having a bad twenty minutes, and they were right back in it because of the penalties we were conceding. We had too much belief in ourselves to panic, though. I felt that if we just played through the phases we'd eventually get another penalty – and the way Ronan was kicking that was going to mean three points. We had a lot of confidence in our defence as well. We knew that fellas would back each other to the death to stop them scoring a try.

PAUL O'CONNELL: We'd brought in a new lineout formation – Hayes and Stringer lifting Donncha at the front. Hayes did all the lifting. When you go in with a formation that they've never seen before, it takes them two or three lineouts to get organized, and that one worked well for us. Donners took a lot of ball – he was playing really well. I didn't feel the ankle at the time, but it probably did slow me down and affect my spring. The ball we won was a bit sloppy. There were some one-handed swat-backs, which aren't ideal. But we tidied things up in the end.

DONNCHA O'CALLAGHAN: People said Paulie must have been carrying his ankle because more balls were thrown to me. But the reason that happened was because it was on – they were marking him more than me. They had so much respect for him that they probably had two guys on him.

We'd done so much work on their lineouts that we knew them inside out. We pride ourselves on picking off one or two balls against oppositions, but early on you could tell it was going to be hard to get close to one. Sometimes you have to put your hand up and say that they've got an extremely good lineout.

Our main concern was winning our own ball. The backs like the ball at the tail – crisp and down to Strings – but sometimes Strings had to get the ball off a maul. So pure respect to Biarritz for that. Even when I managed to steal one from them, about fifteen minutes into the second half, they tore into us and won the ball back. Mistakes were being made by both sides, but we were on the back foot then. We'd lost a bit of momentum.

> **OUR MAIN CONCERN WAS WINNING OUR OWN BALL. THE BACKS LIKE THE BALL AT THE TAIL — CRISP AND DOWN TO STRINGS — BUT SOMETIMES STRINGS HAD TO GET THE BALL OFF A MAUL. SO PURE RESPECT TO BIARRITZ FOR THAT.**

ANTHONY HORGAN: The clock was going so bloody slow. I was looking up every chance I got going, 'Will you please come on, clock. Move it!' Mentally and physically, it was very hard to enjoy yourself out there because it was so close. When they came back at us there was a fear there – a fear that we were going to end up with nothing. When you've lost big matches and things are starting to go against you, there's a little part of you that can think, 'This is just not for us.' You've got to get that thought out of your mind and concentrate on doing your job.

About sixty minutes into it, there was a break in play, and all of a sudden we heard a big roar all around the ground. I looked around me and I thought, 'Jesus – who's coming on here?' Then I saw the big screen – thousands of people massed together in O'Connell Street in Limerick, watching a big screen there. I swear to God it was a massive kick to see it. That helped us, no doubt. It really did make a difference.

KEVIN MITCHELL, *OBSERVER*: The suspicion that there are only two sorts of people on this earth – the Irish and those who want to be – was eerily underscored when the big screen in the stadium flashed up a packed main street of Limerick, and Cardiff was deafened in a roar that reached across the Irish Sea.

PAUL O'CONNELL: We'd gone into a bit of a lull, and the supporters had gone a bit quiet too. They couldn't have been enjoying it at that stage. We needed something to happen – someone make a massive break or a big tackle. Anything to lift us again. It turned out that we got it from the supporters watching the big screen in Limerick.

MARCUS HORAN: Some of the lads were slow to comment on it after the game because

they didn't want to admit they weren't concentrating on the match. But we've spoken about it since and it was something we will remember for ever.

DECLAN KIDNEY: You can get ten people looking at the same thing and there might be ten different ways of looking at it. When the flash of Limerick came up, my reaction was, 'Oh my God – I cannot get wrapped up in this. I cannot get distracted or I'm letting them down. Concentrate on the game.' Everyone could see the way it was going. We had tightened up a bit, and when you're playing the game around the halfway line, or just inside our half, one or two penalties are always going to come.

We knew Marcus was going to tire. By all laws of physiology, he should have been off earlier. You have a lot of time to pick the team you want, and if they're going well you let them see it through. But Marcus had to be suffering. They had already made three substitutions at that stage. So it was time to bring Freddie on.

FEDERICO PUCCIARIELLO: I came on, and it was a difficult time of the game. Then they got another penalty, and Yachvili scored again. It's 20–19 and there's eleven minutes left in the game. Eleven minutes – huge time! I know – everyone knows – that if there is any mistake we lose the final. So I had to focus on my position. Focus. So every scrum – perfectly. If I tackle – roll away immediately. In my career I lost so many finals and semi-finals. I said to myself, 'I cannot accept losing any more.'

JOHN HAYES: The boys were saying, 'Let's not be playing inside our own twenty-two. Let's get down their side of the field – they can't kick from down there.' I wasn't actually saying it. I wouldn't say a whole lot.

PETER STRINGER: We were trying to get the balance right between not sitting back and being too ambitious. We didn't want to be throwing the ball around too much, risking an intercept or turning it over out wide. There was no reason to panic. We had good trust in our defensive system, and guys knew their job.

MARCUS HORAN: It was absolute hell on the bench. I didn't watch much of it – I had my head in my hands. You've got great faith in the boys, but it was torture. I was sitting

'There was no reason to panic': Peter Stringer

there going, 'That clock isn't ticking at all! I looked up at that five minutes ago and it's only moved on two minutes!' It was wrecking my head. With ten minutes to go I copped that every time there was a break in play they stopped the clock. I realized that when it turned eighty minutes it was over.

MICK O'DRISCOLL: With ten minutes to go, I was told I was going on for Axel. Biarritz had made five changes, and at that stage we'd made one. Our pack were playing against four sets of fresh legs, they'd gone through a huge volume of work, and I think it was just a case of freshening it up a bit. I was just delighted to get on the pitch. In that situation, you have to get into it straight away. You can't be tentative.

ANTHONY FOLEY: I saw Micko coming over, and he was going, 'Number eight' – so that was me. You're always disappointed to be called ashore, but obviously we've enough faith in Deccie to know that he's making the decisions for the right reasons. I wouldn't be arrogant enough to think that I can play seventy minutes of rugby at that level and still be better than an international player on the bench who's fresh.

DAVID WALLACE: At 20–19 we were under serious pressure. We'd said it at half-time that they were going to have a good patch and now we just had to deal with it as best we

'Stay tall and follow through'

could, try to create a break for ourselves and then make the most of it. We got into their half and then Johnson was pinged for coming in from the side. Straight away everyone on the pitch thought, 'This is a big moment.'

SHAUN PAYNE: I couldn't watch, I was so nervous. I realized the importance of being four points ahead. I knew if Yachvili got another chance, he could win it for them. I was standing behind the poles when he kicked those three penalties and I was just willing them to go wide, but every one of them was straight over the middle. It was so frustrating. When Rog lined his penalty up, I was thinking, 'This is absolutely vital. Rog, just knock this one over. Please. Just get us four points in front.'

TOM ENGLISH, *SCOTLAND ON SUNDAY*: A sort of calm descended on the Millennium Stadium as O'Gara prepared, and then the big screens behind both goals flashed up the scenes on O'Connell Street again. Absent friends. United in their passion and, in this moment, their anxiety. The noise level went from silence to deafening in a second. There was an eruption all around the ground. Then, they all stared down on O'Gara and waited for that kick.

RONAN O'GARA: It was obvious how important it was, but I just had to get into my routine and block everything else out. Usually there's a mark in the centre of the crossbar and I focus on that. Thomond Park has a black dot, at Lansdowne Road it's green. I imagine a little hoop between the sticks, like a gymnasium hoop, and I picture the ball going through that. I stepped back and the buzz words in my head were, 'Stay tall and follow through.'

DENIS WALSH, *THE SUNDAY TIMES*: Munster had endured twenty minutes of sapping pressure, they had surrendered all of their first-half momentum, they hadn't scored for thirty minutes, their lead was down to a point and the game was on the line. O'Gara? He had committed more errors in the previous ten minutes than he had for the first sixty. A bottler might have choked it. He nailed it.

JOHN KELLY: That was a major lift for us, but we still had seven minutes left. One try in the corner and we were gone. Fair play to them, they gave it absolutely everything. They're a very proud team, like ourselves. Some French sides don't travel well, but these guys turned up big-time.

IAN DOWLING: The only thing in my mind was, 'I don't want to be the one that makes the mistake. Whatever comes my way, I'm going to deal with it.' The place was crazy, but we had to keep our concentration. We had to keep telling each other, 'We're going to get through this and we're going to come out on top.'

TREVOR HALSTEAD: It was nerve-racking. I had a chilling feeling inside of me that they could score a five-pointer. You always fear it's going to get snatched away from you in the last seconds. And it was perfect for a try to win by one point. It's one mistake, one missed tackle. In other games maybe I'd trust someone to make a tackle – not this time. I was keeping an extra eye on them. If something went wrong, I was going to

'I'm going to deal with it': Ian Dowling

be there. I would hate the feeling that it was me who made the mistake that cost us the final – and I wouldn't want anyone else to have that same feeling.

At that stage I was tired but I thought, 'There is no way in hell that they are getting through. I don't care if I have to run left to right forty times to chase, they are not getting through.' Everyone in our team felt exactly the same. We were just telling each other, 'Just keep it up, keep it up, everyone up – let's finish this off.'

DONNCHA O'CALLAGHAN: I don't want to sound cocky or disrespectful, but I just knew after they scored that first try that they weren't going to get another one. Fellas were climbing over each other to get at them. When Rog was standing over that penalty I felt it was incredibly important because they had players who can knock over drop

'You start thinking, "What good am I now?"': Paul O'Connell, who came into the match carrying an ankle knock, comes off late with a hip stinger and leg cramp

goals from anywhere on the pitch. I'm not saying I relaxed for a second. All I'm saying is that I would have been an awful lot more nervous if one kick was all they needed.

PAUL O'CONNELL: Near the end, just after Rog kicked the last penalty, I got a stinger on my hip and I was beginning to cramp a bit. I ran across then and caught the drop-off, and the hip was hindering me. When I was getting treatment I told Kirsty [Peacock] that someone should get warmed up just in case. I'd jumped at a few lineouts before that and the leg was cramping, so you start thinking, 'What good am I now?'

The next lineout was called on me. I jumped and my calf cramped on me again. So then I was thinking, 'If I have to make a tackle or turn and face someone and I cramp again then it could be game over.' So it was time to get off the field.

> **I DON'T WANT TO SOUND COCKY OR DISRESPECTFUL, BUT I JUST KNEW AFTER THEY SCORED THAT FIRST TRY THAT THEY WEREN'T GOING TO GET ANOTHER ONE. FELLAS WERE CLIMBING OVER EACH OTHER TO GET AT THEM.**

ALAN QUINLAN: With six minutes to go I got the call from Jerry Holland to get ready. I was just buzzing. For a couple of seconds, as I was warming up, I thought about all the hard work that I put in on my own in the gym. I was being selfish thinking about it, but I thought deep down that I deserved this, for what I went through. I was proud that I was coming on the field for Munster in a Heineken Cup final. I couldn't get out there fast enough. I wanted to give my all in the time that was left.

DECLAN KIDNEY: When Anthony came off we had Paul there as captain. No problem. Then Paul was wrecked, and we had a bit of a problem. You need a captain on the pitch, somebody with the quality and strength of mind to take responsibility for decisions. Sometimes you just need a fella in there saying, 'Well done.' Mick O'Driscoll is a good man in that situation, so I sent word down: 'Let Quinny tell Micko he's captain.'

ANTHONY FOLEY: Paulie came off and sat down beside me. There was no talk between us whatsoever. Paulie was knackered. I was knackered. We were just sitting there, literally numb. The whole occasion had been so hyped and now all we could do was watch and hope that the boys saw it through.

DONNCHA O'CALLAGHAN: Near the end they kicked a horrible ball down towards Hoggy, and I remember thinking as I was running back, 'This is so important.' Not only did Hoggy take it but he tore into them. He was letting them know that we weren't giving it up.

MICK O'DRISCOLL: With two minutes left they made a break down the right-hand side. They were inside our twenty-two and they had made the gain line by 20 or 30 metres.

236　MUNSTER: OUR ROAD TO GLORY　　　　Opposite: The turf is flying as Denis Leamy presses the attack

Bidabe had it, but two of our backs [John Kelly and Ian Dowling] dragged him to the floor. He offloaded it [to Brusque], and then Trevor made a great tackle, and we got bodies to the ruck.

ANTHONY FOLEY: As the clock got closer to the eighty minutes I stood up. I was just feeling it so much I couldn't sit down. It was hard, but I had tons of confidence in the players out on the field. Donners and John Hayes bursted a fella – there was no way the boys were letting them through.

DENIS LEAMY: Right near the end, about twenty seconds left, they were coming at us again, and we got a lucky decision for offside [against Bobo]. With Axel off, I was at Number 8 when the ref gave the scrum. I told Stringer I was going to get the ball off the pitch the first chance I got. I was going to tap it to myself, run over the line and try to keep the ball. He screamed at me not to. He said, 'No! I'm doing it!'

JOHN HAYES: After they got penalized, one of the boys had a look at Chris White, as if to say, 'Is it over?' I heard him say, 'Ten seconds left.' That meant he was going to play the scrum. We just pulled in together. We knew we had to have a huge scrum because if they turned it over play would continue until they either lost it or scored. I'll tell you what I was thinking at that very second. 'Get in. Get it solid. Get the ball out. Game over.'

JERRY FLANNERY: We had planned this. We knew they were going to have massive scrums at the start and they did. They were massive men. But we were staying the pace and we had something left in the tank at the end, when we needed it. On that final scrum, we just wanted to keep straight. We didn't want to give an angle at all. Straight ball. The scrum is longer when it's straight. Keep it in there and let the clock tick over. Then get it off the pitch.

RYLE NUGENT, RTE COMMENTATOR: Ten seconds. Is this it? After all the years of trying, after all the times that Munster have come so close and failed. Eighty minutes ticks over. Stringer …

Opposite: Mick O'Driscoll, a late substitute for Anthony Foley,
captained Munster for the last four minutes of the match

Jerry Holland looks pensively into the sea of red

PETER STRINGER: Chris White had told me it was over the next time the ball went out of play. Just before I put the ball in at the scrum there was a huge roar from the crowd and I looked up at the clock. It was showing 80:02. I was trying to decide if I should risk passing it to Ronan when the ball came out of the scrum or if should I kick it out myself. Yachvili came right around, trying to stop me from kicking to touch. He was well offside. I couldn't kick it out then because he was standing right in my way.

FEDERICO PUCCIARIELLO: A little mistake in the scrum and we have lost the ball – they can push over. We go in, they go up and we stay in our position. We don't go back. Not one centimetre. They go up, and the referee resets the scrum.

DONNCHA O'CALLAGHAN: When they came up from the scrum it was reset, and we piled into it again. Strings was saying, 'Leave it in there, leave it in there.' He was as calm as you like. As if we were out on the training pitch in Musgrave Park. 'Leave it there lads, leave it there.' He felt we were in control of the situation, and that came through to us. The ball was at the back of the scrum, and we were all working our socks off, but we were comfortable. I swear to God, we were nearly able to enjoy it. I remember thinking about it as I was in there: 'We could nearly leave this there for as long as we need to.'

PETER STRINGER: It was a real solid scrum and it bought us a bit of time. There was no panic. As much as I wanted to get that bloody ball into the stand I thought, 'It's worth another couple of seconds.' So I did nothing and the ref did it all.

FEDERICO PUCCIARIELLO: They tried to turn us on our left side. But we stayed square, like a machine. It was an awesome scrum, at that stage of the game. They split and all their back row were offside.

SHAUN PAYNE: He lifted his arm for a penalty and it was 80:30 on the clock. I thought, 'It's going to go off in one second here …'

DONNCHA O'CALLAGHAN: I just thought, 'It's not over. There'll be injury time. There'll be something.'

MICK O'DRISCOLL: 'That's it. It's all over. Just kick it straight into Row Z.'

JOHN HAYES: 'Get it out of there. The farther up into the crowd the better.'

PETER STRINGER: Denis was standing there with the ball in his hands. There was a second or two where people weren't sure if it was over or not. But I knew we just had to kick it out.

DENIS LEAMY: I was about to get it off the pitch when he robbed it off me. Tore it out of my hands. Robbed me of my glory moment.

PETER STRINGER: I wasn't taking any chances. We'd waited long enough for this to happen. I wanted it to be over. I was thinking, 'Come on, give it to me, I'll do it.' Bang. Into the stand. And then he blew the final whistle.

I'd thought about it before the game – what I would do if we won. I wasn't planning it – just trying to imagine what it would feel like. But you can't. When the whistle went I started jumping around, and then it just hit me.

We've won the European Cup.

Being honest, there was a part of me that didn't think it would ever happen. I went

down on my knees and got very emotional. It just overtook me, overwhelmed me. Everything I'd been through with this team, all those thoughts, all those emotions, all those dreams, all those times where I lay awake trying to put right what went wrong in the other matches, but it can never change. The feeling you get when it does go right, when it does actually happen … Jesus, I don't know how to put it into words.

JOHN HAYES: I looked over and saw the Biarritz fellas. I felt sorry for them. Some of them were lying down, some of them were on their hands and knees, bent over. I thought, 'Don't worry, lads, I fucking know how that feels.' I shook hands with a lot of them. It was important to do that.

RONAN O'GARA: I was so happy I couldn't believe it. It was the realization of something we had worked so hard for, and there was huge satisfaction in that. I was in a world of my own and I couldn't have been happier at that moment.

ANTHONY FOLEY: Everyone on the bench charged across the pitch. We just wanted to get the party started. We'd been labelled as bridesmaids and we were sick of it. People said we'd never win it, we'd always be second-best. It goes back to the bitterness and pride. We'd shoved it down those people's throats.

PAUL O'CONNELL: I ran towards the team and all of a sudden I was in tears. You don't realize the cameras are on you and I cringed when I saw it later, but it was just a crazy,

Shaun Payne, Ronan O'Gara and Alan Quinlan

> **EVERYONE ON THE BENCH CHARGED ACROSS THE PITCH. WE JUST WANTED TO GET THE PARTY STARTED. WE'D BEEN LABELLED AS BRIDESMAIDS AND WE WERE SICK OF IT. PEOPLE SAID WE'D NEVER WIN IT, WE'D ALWAYS BE SECOND-BEST. IT GOES BACK TO THE BITTERNESS AND PRIDE. WE'D SHOVED IT DOWN THOSE PEOPLE'S THROATS.**

surreal day, full of emotion. Stephen Keogh, a great character and a great friend of mine who has moved to Leinster now, came around to us all before the match with big tears in his eyes, wishing us well. That was the start of the emotion. Most of those guys will be friends for life. I don't know how many other teams are like that. For a minute it got on top of me, but then I got myself together.

You invest so much of your life in rugby. Relationships are up or down depending on what happens, and maybe that's something we all need to look at. It's hard on the people around us, and we find it tough to disconnect from it. Your happiness shouldn't depend on eighty minutes on a Saturday afternoon. But at the moment, for a lot of us, it does. So when you get a day like that, something you've been striving for, and the people who mean the most to you are there to see it and share it with you, I don't think sport can ever get any better.

DENIS LEAMY: It's not very often you get rewarded for all your hard work. Sometimes you deserve a lot better and you don't get it. But when you do win something like that, the feeling is incredible. I don't think you can get it in any other walk of life.

Most of my happiness was for my family. I thought as well about the guys who lost the two finals, the players in the team before me who played a massive part in getting us to this position. As a young fella I watched them on TV and felt for them. When I saw people crying with happiness in the stand I thought about what it meant to them. And I thought about Conrad. To be honest, he's never that far away from my thoughts.

SHAUN PAYNE: I cried. Absolutely I cried. I've only been here three seasons, and you can see what it meant to me. How many times do you have to multiply that to get a measure of how much it meant to guys like Axel? I'd hate to think how they would have felt if we had lost, because I would have been destroyed.

DAVID WALLACE: I thought of the people who had travelled with us all these years. The thought of going back without it was too much to bear on your shoulders.

ANTHONY FOLEY: Everyone went mad for a while, and then we settled down. I turned around, and Donners was walking over with my son, Tony. Ah, it was a great moment. He didn't understand what was going on, but we can show it to him in a few years' time. I had him for couple of minutes and then I had to hand him back to Olive, my wife. He was probably happy enough to go back to her because of the smell of sweat off me.

JOHN HAYES: They put up a platform on the pitch, and I could see the cup. I'd been fine up to then, grand and relaxed. But when I saw that yoke out in the middle of the field, I was thinking, 'Come on. Get up them steps and get that cup. I just want to get my hands on it.'

Biarritz had to go through first. I was looking at that, thinking, 'I know what that's like too, lads. Had that twice.' Then we went up and all got our medals. Axel was last up. I was like, 'Will you ever just hand it over to him?' I just wanted to grab it and touch it, because I had never had touched it before.

John Hayes with David Wallace: 'Get up them steps and get that cup'

ANTHONY FOLEY: I was standing there waiting for them to give me the trophy. Everybody in the stadium wanted to get cracking, but they were making me wait. I wanted to lift it so much I was nearly going to go over and just take it. They finally gave it to me and straight away I was surprised how bloody heavy it was. I had never touched it. I'd never asked anybody what it was like. I lifted it up and felt sheer joy. There was just madness in the stands.

JOHN HAYES: I reached out and grabbed it and got a hold of it for one second. I let it off then. Once I had touched it, I didn't mind then. I was thinking, 'That's that done now.' I was happy at that.

MARCUS HORAN: The rest of the squad broke through security on the bottom corner of the pitch. They were all wearing their navy fleeces, and we saw them all sprinting towards us. We just went nuts with them.

BARRY MURPHY: I'd been co-commentator on Limerick radio. I just wanted to say, 'I was commentating with Len Dineen when we won the Heineken Cup' – that's why I did it.

In the press box everyone was sitting down, tipping away on laptops, and the two of us were jumping up and down. A couple of people behind us were telling us to sit down, but we were having none it. Then Len told me, 'Get down there! Get down on to that field!'

I had been careful with the leg for the previous few weeks but I knew I could push it a bit. I ran around the stadium about six times trying to find the right place to go. I begged this security guard to let me in. I told him I was an injured Munster player but I was in a hoodie and a pair of jeans and I could have been anyone. I was showing him my passport, begging him, practically on my knees.

Eventually these fans were walking past. They were saying, 'Go on, Barry!' I said to them, 'Tell him! Tell him I play for Munster!' He let me in at last, and I legged it on to the pitch. Deccie was the first person I saw and I sprinted over to him. He started laughing, pointing at my leg. I still felt very involved. I think everyone did.

> I HAD BEEN CAREFUL WITH THE LEG FOR THE PREVIOUS FEW WEEKS BUT I KNEW I COULD PUSH IT A BIT. I RAN AROUND THE STADIUM ABOUT SIX TIMES TRYING TO FIND THE RIGHT PLACE TO GO. I BEGGED THIS SECURITY GUARD TO LET ME IN. I TOLD HIM I WAS AN INJURED MUNSTER PLAYER BUT I WAS IN A HOODIE AND A PAIR OF JEANS AND I COULD HAVE BEEN ANYONE.

JERRY FLANNERY: When Stringer kicked the ball out it was relief – it wasn't joy. I was happy for myself but I was happy too for my family, friends, coaches, people who had faith in me, the ones who said, 'Keep it going, you're going to get there, you're going to play for Ireland.' To me, this was a bit of payback for those people. At the time I thought, 'How can they believe in me? I'm sitting on the bench for Munster and playing AIL rugby.' I always believed in myself, but everyone needs belief from other people too, no matter what they do in life.

ANTHONY HORGAN: There were some tears. It's hard not to. It was relief I felt, a weight off all our shoulders. There were a lot of things written about me, and there are two ways of taking it – you can lie down and roll over or take it on the chin and bounce back. I'd like to think that, in a small way, I have done that. I have a gold medal in my drawer at home.

DONNCHA O'CALLAGHAN: People talked about feeling just relief, but it wasn't like that for me at all. It was just the greatest feeling that you'd won with your friends in an atmosphere that will never be recreated. Our supporters were just magnificent.

We were all running around with the cup, and Strings said, 'Calm down, slow down, we've got to enjoy this and remember it.' So many people have told me it was the best sporting occasion they were ever at, and when you hear them come out with that you just think, 'I was a part of it and, yes, it was incredible.'

Opposite: Jerry Flannery: 'I always believed in myself, but everyone needs belief from other people too'

Paul O'Connell and Donncha O'Callaghan

I know what it's like to lose and I'd hate it if anyone from Biarritz thought that we rubbed it in, that we tore the arse out of it and made then feel bad or disrespected them. I wanted them to know that we knew what it was like for them.

PAUL O'CONNELL: We were going very slowly around the pitch, and I drank half a bottle of champagne. I don't know why I did that. I suppose it was because we had just gone bananas. We put the trophy in the middle and we all started dancing jigs.

TREVOR HALSTEAD: That pressure was off, and something else was going to take its place. It took a while, but I started to feel great satisfaction with what we had done. When I switched on my phone later the text messages kept coming through for ages, one after the other. My family had been through the lows of losing the finals with me, and I phoned my parents. They watched it at home and they were massively proud and relieved for me. They knew how much not being wanted by the Sharks and the Springboks had hurt me. Yeah, it was all good.

SHAUN PAYNE: A lot of my family had come over from South Africa. I met them outside the tunnel, and it was really special. My dad has been an avid supporter, ever since I started playing the game. He was pretty emotional, for a person who is not emotional at all. He just said, 'This is the best day of my life.' He said he had never experienced anything that came close to it.

Federico Pucciariello

DECLAN KIDNEY: When final whistle went, Brian [Hickey] said to me, 'Come on, let's go, they've got a lift put aside to get us down there.' I'd love to have just watched it from there, even for a little while, but he dragged me away. I remember seeing Tom Kiernan leaving his seat at Lansdowne Road on the day Ulster won it in 1999. I watched him look around at the celebrations. It was a quiet moment for him and he's a private man. I don't know what he was thinking, but he was one of the driving forces behind this tournament and he should have been very proud of instigating a competition like this.

Just before I went into the dressing room, I met him. That was a special moment for me. I think Anthony Foley would call it a manly hug. He was just ecstatic. We didn't say anything. There was nothing to be said. What was going on outside said it all. It meant so much to so many different people.

KILLIAN KEANE: I didn't know how I would feel if they won it. In 2000 I played in the final and in 2002 I played in some of the earlier matches so I would have got a medal if we'd done it. I was afraid that I wouldn't be 100 per cent happy. I was afraid there might be negative feelings: 'I'm not part of this – why couldn't we have won it when I was there?'

Sitting up in the stand, next to Frankie Sheahan and the other injured players, I could feel the emotion rising in me at the final whistle. I was happy for the lads on the pitch. And I was happy that I was happy – if that makes any sense. Happy that all I felt was joy, that there was nothing else – no envy or self-pity. I would have hated that.

Frankie and I hugged – neither of us wanted to pull away from it and when we eventually did both of us were in tears. Then Frankie and the rest of the guys started making for the lift, to get down on to the pitch. I didn't feel right about going down, so I just stood there by myself. There were Munster fans below looking up at me, and I was just standing there, crying. But so happy.

MICK GALWEY: Of course I'd love to have been on the pitch myself, but a lot of people said to me, 'Well done, Mick, this wasn't all about today – this was about a journey.' And I did feel that and I was so proud of the lads for winning it.

I was working for Radio Kerry and at the press conference I saw Declan and Anthony walk in with the cup. I just wanted to go up and congratulate them. I didn't want to be waiting for the end of it – I wanted to get it off my back. So I just said,

> **SITTING UP IN THE STAND, NEXT TO FRANKIE SHEAHAN AND THE OTHER INJURED PLAYERS, I COULD FEEL THE EMOTION RISING IN ME AT THE FINAL WHISTLE. I WAS HAPPY FOR THE LADS ON THE PITCH. AND I WAS HAPPY THAT I WAS HAPPY — IF THAT MAKES ANY SENSE. HAPPY THAT ALL I FELT WAS JOY, THAT THERE WAS NOTHING ELSE — NO ENVY OR SELF-PITY. I WOULD HAVE HATED THAT.**

'Go on, Foley, you good thing!' He called me up there and we had a bit of a hug. I knew what it meant to Anthony Foley, Anthony Foley knew what it meant to me.

KEITH WOOD: Guys who were under pressure during the season came up trumps on the final day, and that was very heartening to see. At the end of it I was ecstatic for Foley, who had a tough year. He deserved it – and I don't use that expression lightly. People say, 'Ah, your man is the best player never to get a cap.' I've always said, 'Well, if he didn't get a cap he didn't deserve to.' But if any man deserved to get the bloody European Cup it was Foley. Yes, he absolutely did deserve it.

Some people said to me, 'God, you must be sad that you're not out there, Woody.' And I just thought, 'But this is all I wanted. Why would I possibly be sad?' I met Hugo MacNeill, and he said it was quite comfortably the best sporting occasion he had ever been to in his life.

Before that match, I would never have said that the Munster team was great. Great supporters and everything else, but they weren't a great team. They hadn't earned the right to be called great. People are too liberal with that word. But now it's justified. They achieved that by taking the trophy after all those years, all those games. They are a great team. I felt honoured to be there to witness it.

John Hayes finds a quiet place for a phone call

No Munster supporter wanted to leave. They had waited too long. They had
experienced many emotions that afternoon, but in the end, as the players walked
slowly around the perimeter of the pitch and thrilled in the moment with them,
the most powerful was joy.

Finally, as their supporters sang along to 'We Are The Champions', the Munster
players began making their way down the tunnel. One of them had already left the stage.
Donncha O'Callaghan had slipped away a few minutes before. He wanted a little time
to himself. He walked to the corner of the dressing room and took a small white jar

out of his bag and opened it. Inside was the holy cross he had found on the school rugby pitch many years before. He took the tiny cross out of the jar and held it between the thumb and index finger of his right hand. Then he fell to his knees and prayed.

When the rest of the Munster squad and the back-room staff arrived, they gathered together in the middle of the dressing room. Eighteen of them had joined the battle on the pitch, but there were close on three times that number there now, arm in arm, and all of them had played a part in winning the trophy that was sitting on top of a small plastic skip in front of them, a Munster flag tied around it.

They sang two choruses of their anthem, 'Stand Up And Fight', and for the second

Donncha O'Callaghan, the first player back in the dressing room, gives thanks

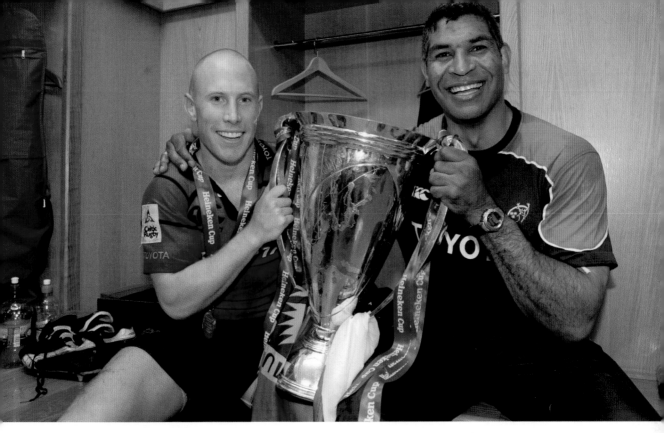

Peter Stringer and Jim Williams

they stamped their feet off the floor and fired beer at each other. Peter Clohessy, who had been in tears in the same changing room four years before, when his career ended with bitter defeat in the final against Leicester, was the favourite target of the beer-throwers. He stood there smiling, with Rob Henderson on one side of him and Ian Dowling on the other. There was a dazed expression on Dowling's face. Four days later it was unchanged.

Barry Murphy, the young centre whose season was so cruelly cut short by injury, sat in a corner while a photograph was being taken of the players with medals around their necks. He was thinking to himself, 'I wish I was in there with ye.' Recognizing the thought, John Kelly broke away and walked towards him. He took the Number 13 jersey off his back and handed it to Murphy.

'Here,' he said. 'I was only minding it for you.'

Opposite top: The squad sings 'Stand Up and Fight'
Opposite middle: Anthony Foley and Peter Clohessy
Opposite bottom: O'Connell, Leamy and Jeremy Manning

MUNSTER: OUR ROAD TO GLORY 263

EPILOGUE
BRINGING IT ALL BACK HOME

❝ WE ACHIEVED SOMETHING SPECIAL BUT IT'S TIME TO MOVE ON. ❞

Flight DK3094 arrived at Shannon airport just before 1 a.m. Five thousand people were packed into the concourse to welcome the heroes home. DK himself – an emotional Declan Kidney – led them in another rendition of 'The Fields Of Athenry', the anthem that had raised the roof in Cardiff when the clock was stuck on 78:50 and the Munster supporters dared to dream. For good measure, Kidney followed it with 'Stand Up And Fight'.

When he eventually left the party at the Clarion hotel in Limerick, Anthony Foley took the cup up to his room. There was a ledge over the bed, and he left it there for what remained of the night. When he woke that morning and saw it sitting above his head he thought, 'There it is. It wasn't a dream.'

The open-top bus began its journey through the city at 4 p.m. the following day. It being Limerick in May, the rain arrived on cue, and the players scrambled for umbrellas as the bus turned into the parish of St Mary's, heartland of Limerick rugby. Another enormous crowd was waiting for them on O'Connell Street, where the big screen that had allowed Munster supporters in Limerick and Cardiff to wave to each other was still in place. Hardier souls walked every step of the route alongside the bus and for them the smallest man on board was the biggest hero of all.

'Stringer! Throw me down an umbrella!'

'Stringer! Can I have your tie?'

'Aboy Stringer! Some bit of stuff, isn't he?'

PETER STRINGER: Liverpool are my soccer team. I've got a video at home of the day they said goodbye to the terrace on the Kop. The fans were chanting the names of great players from the past, guys who had long gone but were fondly remembered.

When you hear people shouting out your own name you feel humble. It's an unbelievable feeling that people respect you enough to say your name in unison.

People said to me, 'You really showed them, the ones who said those things a bout you.' But I don't feel the need to react to people outside the group who have been negative about the team or about me personally. I'm just glad that I have experienced this and been part of it. That's enough for me.

JOHN KELLY: That week myself and Stringer took the cup out to our old school, St Anthony's in Ballinlough. The kids went mental when they saw it. There are a lot of good memories, but that one is right up there.

MARCUS HORAN: My old school, St Munchin's in Limerick, had won the Munster Senior Schools Cup a few months earlier. Five days after the final I went out there with Axel and Jerry Flannery. We never won it ourselves when we were there. Axel still talks about the pain of losing that final. He was captain, and the school was in mourning for a week. No matter what heights you get to, things like that will always haunt you. But now, we had both cups together – ours and theirs.

JERRY FLANNERY: We came back to Limerick and went around to bars like Cowhey's and Charlie St George's, the Office and the Roundhouse, and my dad's place. We had the cup with us, and to see sixty-year-old men crying when they held it – Jesus Christ. They're the real old characters in Limerick and they've seen so much rugby in their lifetimes you feel you want to impress them. I was just very proud to go around to all those places because there's a history and a tradition in this town that means a lot. To feel that you are part of that now is one of the best things about winning. Rugby will always be strong in Limerick, there will always be new players coming through. But now people will remember my time – when I got to mind the Munster jersey for a while.

Opposite top: Paul O'Connell with admirers at the team hotel in Limerick
Opposite middle: 'Stringer! Can I have your tie?': the Limerick homecoming
Opposite bottom: Rob Henderson with his daughter Mia

MUNSTER: OUR ROAD TO GLORY   267

Declan Kidney hoists the cup at the Cork homecoming

DECLAN KIDNEY: One of the biggest things that struck me afterwards was the generosity of all the past players. It would be the most natural thing in the world to feel left out, but there was genuine delight. It's very rare in life that you get so much of that from everybody.

Three weeks after the final I had some time to myself and I sat down and put on a tape of the match. I didn't realize how much we had cocooned ourselves from it. I was surprised by how much it affected me.

ROB HENDERSON: After all the celebrations, the last [Celtic League] match of the season was against Cardiff at Thomond Park that Saturday. It was my last day as a Munster player. It was the same for some other lads – Mike Mullins, Stephen Keogh, Trevor Hogan, Paul Burke, Mike Prendergast. I have no idea how, but we hockeyed Cardiff. Half of our team were in need of a new kidney, but that attitude was still there: 'OK,

I'm not going to let you down, you don't let me down and neither of us want to let the supporters down.'

I remember saying to myself, 'Right, this is your last match – don't try and do too much, just do what you're good at.' I played well and enjoyed myself. It would have been nice to have scored a little meat-pie at the end, but it wasn't to be. Then, suddenly, it's all over. We went into the changing room afterwards and I'd be lying if I said there weren't a few tears under the stand. I thought, 'That's it – I won't play with the lads again.' Then we got called back into the stand, one by one, and we all lifted the trophy and had a bit of a sing-song. It was a fitting way to finish, in front of a packed Thomond Park.

PAUL O'CONNELL: Everyone could see the bond between the team and the supporters that day in Cardiff, and I'm glad they all dined out on it – but they can't let their expectations slide now that we've won one European Cup. We have a lot more to achieve, and the beauty of the relationship between the players and the supporters is the pressure they put us under. If that expectation goes – if the supporters settle for having won it once, if they start dwelling on past glories – then we won't be half of what we were.

I want to see them raise their ambitions for us. If the players don't feel that pressure, small things will creep in and hurt us. The foot will go off the pedal a little bit. You only need to drop from one hundred per cent to ninety-nine to start losing your footing. We achieved something special, but it's time to move on, to keep driving on as if we've never won it. That's what winners do.

ANTHONY FOLEY: We've got a big bullseye on our jerseys now that we're the European champions, but that's a good thing. There's hard work ahead of us.

This isn't the time to look back on what we achieved in Cardiff, but that time will come for all of us. When it does, we'll sit back and say, 'Yes, that was a nice day, that was a nice feeling. It was good to do that in front of all those people and it was good to be involved with such a great bunch of lads.'

Overleaf: Following the Celtic League match the Saturday after the Heineken Cup final, the fans crowded on to the Thomond Park pitch for another singsong with the trophy

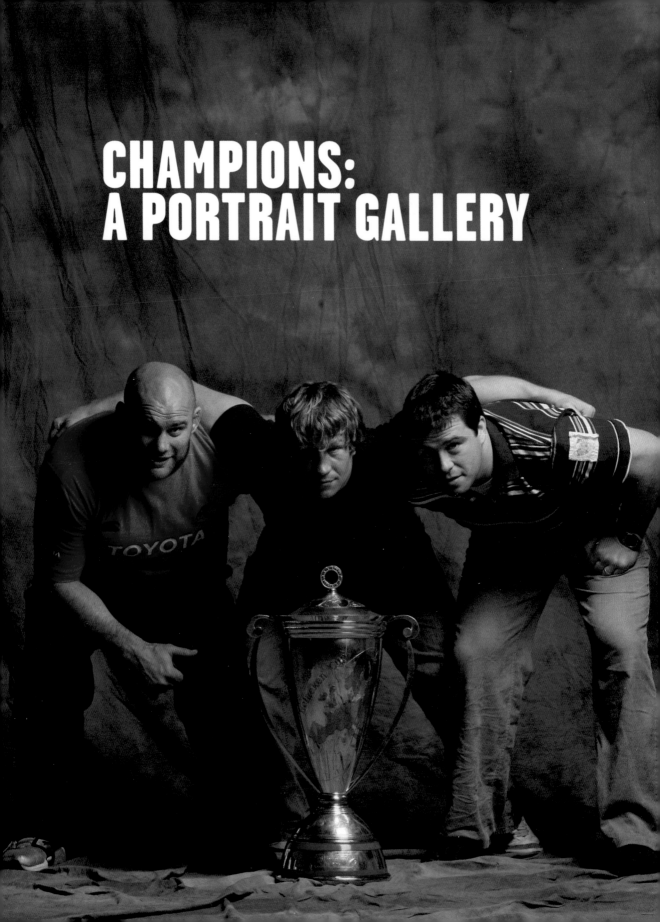

CHAMPIONS: A PORTRAIT GALLERY

Opposite: The front row: John Hayes, Jerry Flannery, Marcus Horan
This page: The second row: Donncha O'Callaghan, Paul O'Connell

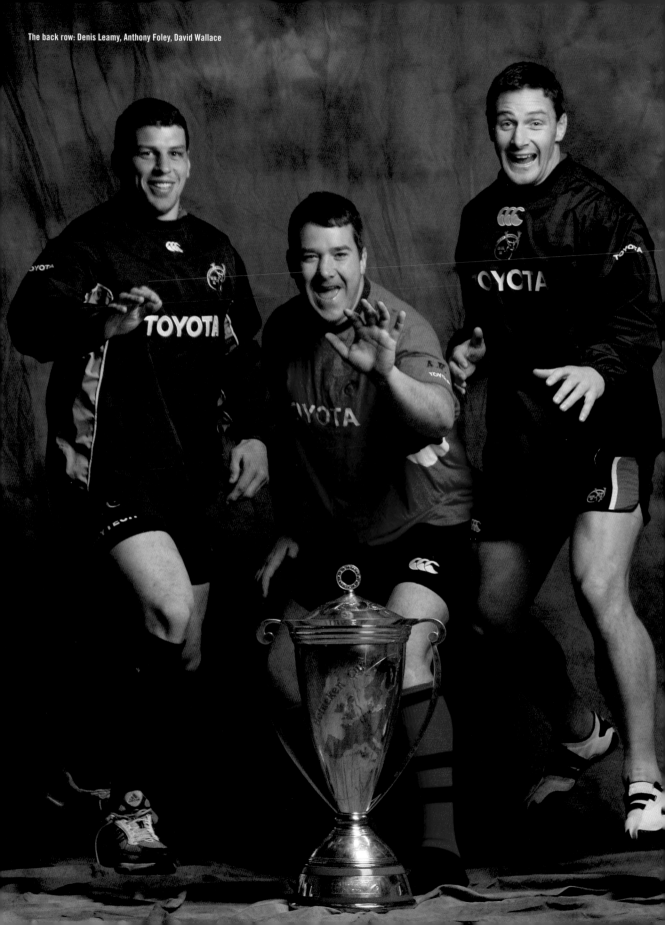

The back row: Denis Leamy, Anthony Foley, David Wallace

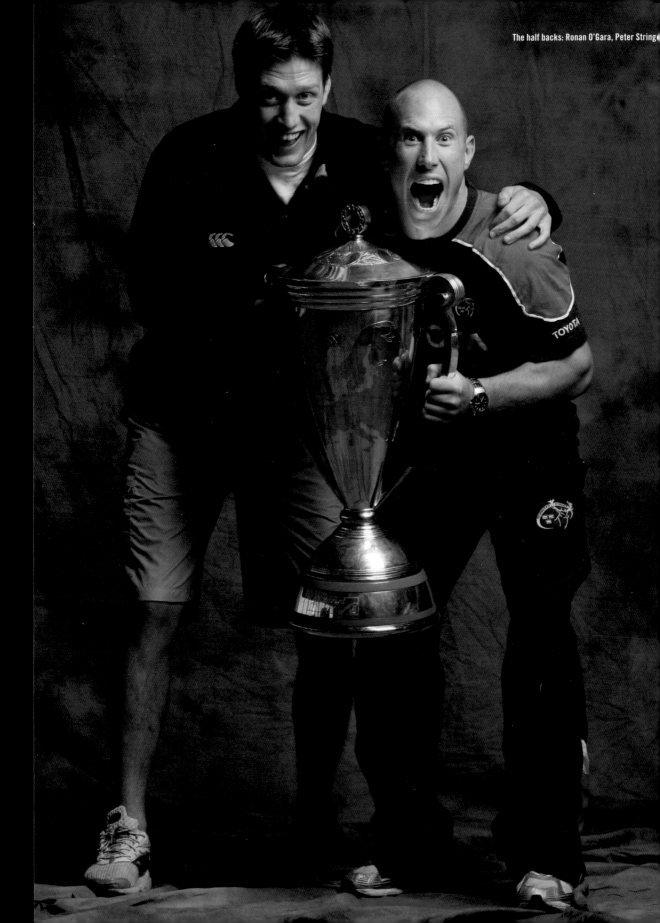

The centres: John Kelly, Trevor Halstead

The back three: Ian Dowling, Shaun Payne, Anthony Horgan

The subs: Alan Quinlan, Mick O'Driscoll, Denis Fogarty, Jeremy Manning, Rob Henderson, Federico Pucciarello, Tomás O'Leary

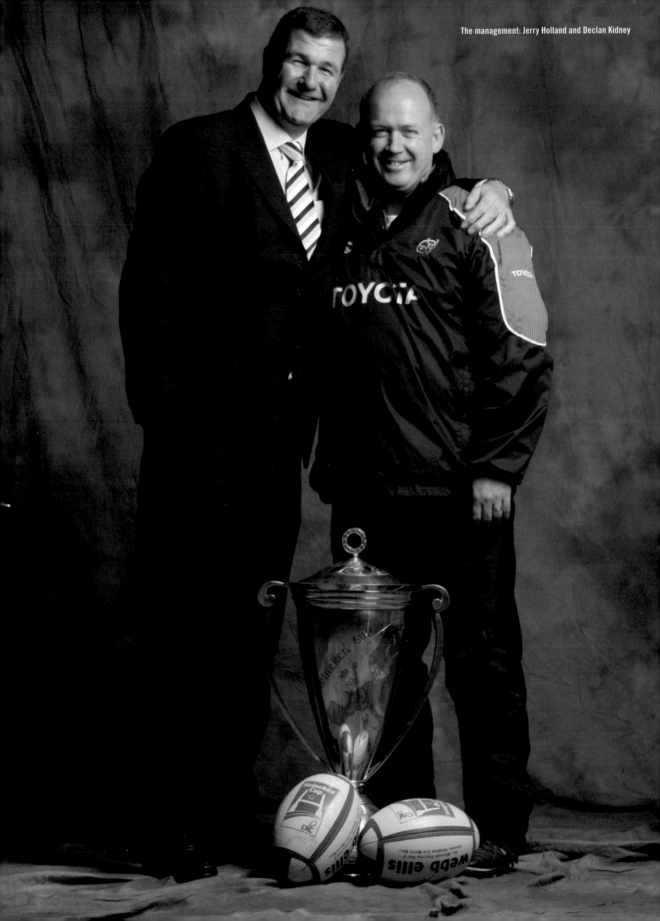

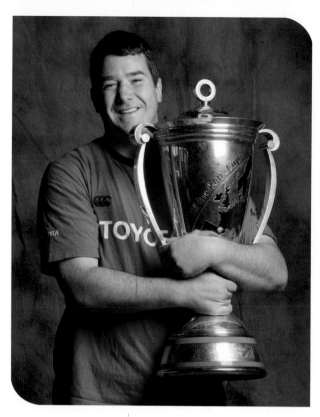

The captain: Anthony Foley

The coach: Declan Kidney

The coaching staff: Jim Williams, Paul McCarthy, Brian Hickey, Tony McGahan

The fitness team: Feargal O'Callaghan, Damien Mednis, Sean Whitney, Aidan O'Connell (sitting)

The physio team: Dave Revins, Kirsty Peacock, Nick Green

The medical team: Michael Shinkwin, Eanna Falvey, Tadhg O'Sullivan

The operations team: Pat Geraghty, Jack Kiely, Bryan Murphy, George Murray

The CEO: Garret Fitzgerald

APPENDIX: MUNSTER'S RECORD IN THE HEINEKEN EUROPEAN CUP, 1995–2006

* Played at Musgrave Park. All other home matches played at Thomond Park.

1995–1996
Pool stage

1 November 1995 Munster 17 Swansea 13
8 November 1995 Castres Olympique 19 Munster 12
Munster did not qualify for knockout stages

1996–1997
Pool stage

12 October 1996 Munster 23 Milan 5*
16 October 1996 Cardiff Blues 48 Munster 18
19 October 1996 Munster 49 London Wasps 22
2 November 1996 Toulouse 60 Munster 19
Munster did not qualify for knockout stages

1997–1998
Pool stage

7 September 1997 NEC Harlequins 48 Munster 40
13 September 1997 Cardiff Blues 43 Munster 23
20 September 1997 Munster 17 Bourgoin 15
27 September 1997 Munster 32 Cardiff Blues 37*
4 October 1997 Bourgoin 21 Munster 6
12 October 1997 Munster 23 NEC Harlequins 16
Munster did not qualify for knockout stages

1998–1999
Pool stage

19 September 1998 Munster 20 Padova 13*
26 September 1998 Munster 34 Neath 10*
10 October 1998 Perpignan 41 Munster 24
17 October 1998 Neath 18 Munster 18
31 October 1998 Munster 13 Perpignan 5*
8 November 1998 Padova 21 Munster 35

Quarter-final

13 December 1998 Colomiers 23 Munster 9
Munster: B Roche; J O'Neill, K Keane, R Ellison, M Lynch; B Everitt, P Stringer; P Clohessy, M McDermott, J Hayes; M Galwey (capt), M O'Driscoll; D Corkery, A Foley, E Halvey. **Replacements:** D Clohessy for Hayes (half-time), T Tierney for Stringer (58 mins), D Wallace for Corkery (65 mins), S Leahy for O'Driscoll (76 mins).
Munster scorer: Penalties: Keane (3)

1999–2000
Pool stage

20 November 1999 Munster 32 Pontypridd 10
28 November 1999 Saracens 34 Munster 35
11 December 1999 Colomiers 15 Munster 31
18 December 1999 Munster 23 Colomiers 5*
8 January 2000 Munster 31 Saracens 30
15 January 2000 Pontypridd 38 Munster 36

Quarter-final

15 April 2000 Munster 27 Stade Français 10
Munster: D Crotty; J Kelly, M Mullins, K Keane, A Horgan; R O'Gara, P Stringer; P Clohessy, K Wood, J Hayes; M Galwey (capt), J Langford; E Halvey, A Foley, D Wallace. **Replacements:** M Horan for Hayes (25 mins), A Quinlan for Halvey (80 mins).
Munster scorers: Tries: Horgan, Crotty; Conversion: O'Gara; Penalties: O'Gara (5)

Semi-final

6 May 2000 Toulouse 25 Munster 31
Munster: D Crotty; J Kelly, M Mullins, J Holland, A Horgan; R O'Gara, P Stringer; P Clohessy, K Wood, J Hayes; M Galwey (capt), J Langford; E Halvey, A Foley, D Wallace. **Replacements:** F Sheahan for Wood (half-time), M Horan for Hayes (73 mins), D O'Callaghan for Galwey (78 mins).
Munster scorers: Tries: Hayes, O'Gara, Holland; Conversions: O'Gara (2); Penalties: O'Gara (4)

Final

27 May 2000 Northampton 9 Munster 8
Northampton: P Grayson; C Moir, A Bateman, M Allen, B Cohen; A Hepher, D Malone; G Pagel, F Mendez, M Stewart; A Newman, T Rodber; D Mackinnon, P Lam (capt), B Poutney. **Replacements:** M Szelzo for Stewart (68 mins), J Fillis for Newman (71 mins), J Brannall for Malone (74 mins).
Munster: D Crotty; J Kelly, M Mullins, J Holland, A Horgan; R O'Gara, P Stringer; P Clohessy, K Wood, J Hayes; M Galwey (capt), J Langford; E Halvey, A Foley, D Wallace. **Replacements:** K Keane for Crotty (80 mins).
Northampton scorer: Penalties: Grayson (3)
Munster scorers: Try: Wallace; Drop goal: Holland

2000–2001

Pool stage

7 October 2000 Munster 26 Newport 18

14 October 2000 Castres Olympique 29 Munster 32

21 October 2000 Munster 31 Bath 9

28 October 2000 Bath 18 Munster 5

13 January 2001 Newport 24 Munster 39

20 January 2001 Munster 21 Castres Olympique 11*

Quarter-final

28 January 2001 Munster 38 Biarritz Olympique 29

Munster: D Crotty; J Kelly, M Mullins, J Holland, A Horgan; R O'Gara, P Stringer; P Clohessy, F Sheahan, J Hayes; M Galwey, J Langford, A Quinlan; A Foley, D Wallace. **Replacements:** none.

Munster scorers: Tries: Foley (3); Conversion: O'Gara; Penalties: O'Gara (7)

Semi-final

21 April 2001 Stade Français 16 Munster 15

Munster: D Crotty; J O'Neill, M Mullins, J Holland, A Horgan; R O'Gara, P Stringer; P Clohessy, F Sheahan, J Hayes; M Galwey (capt), J Langford; D O'Callaghan, A Foley, D Wallace. **Replacements:** D O Cuinneagain for O'Callaghan (70 mins), M Horan for Clohessy (80 mins).

Munster scorer: Penalties: O'Gara (5)

2001–2002

Pool stage

29 September 2001 Munster 28 Castres Olympique 23

6 October 2001 NEC Harlequins 8 Munster 24

26 October 2001 Bridgend 12 Munster 16

3 November 2001 Munster 40 Bridgend 6*

5 January 2002 Munster 51 NEC Harlequins 17

12 January 2002 Castres Olympique 21 Munster 13

Quarter-final

26 January 2002 Stade Français 14 Munster 16

Munster: D Crotty; J Kelly, R Henderson, J Holland, A Horgan; R O'Gara, P Stringer; P Clohessy, F Sheahan, J Hayes, M Galwey (capt), P O'Connell, J Williams, A Foley, D Wallace. **Replacements:** M Horan for Hayes (temp 6–14 mins), Horan for Clohessy (80 mins).

Munster scorers: Try: Horgan; Conversion: O'Gara; Penalties: O'Gara (2), Drop goal: O'Gara

Semi-final

27 April 2005 Castres Olympique 17 Munster 25

Munster: D Crotty; J Kelly, R Henderson, J Holland, A Horgan; R O'Gara, P Stringer; P Clohessy, F Sheahan, J Hayes; M Galwey (capt), P O'Connell; A Quinlan, A Foley, D Wallace. **Replacements:** D O'Callaghan for Foley (16 mins), M Horan for O'Callaghan (temp 23–30 mins) and for Clohessy (70 mins), M Mullins for O'Gara

(temp 46–52 mins) and for Henderson (80 mins), J Staunton for Crotty (80 mins). **Sin-binned:** Clohessy (20 mins).

Munster scorers: Try: Kelly; Conversion: O'Gara; Penalties: O'Gara (6)

Final

25 May 2002 Leicester Tigers 15 Munster 9

Leicester Tigers: T Stimpson; G Murphy, O Smith, R Kafer, F Tuilagi; A Healey, J Hamilton; G Rowntree, D West, D Garforth; M Johnson (capt), B Kay; L Moody, M Corry, N Back. **Replacements:** H Ellis for Hamilton (52 mins), P Freshwater for Garforth (74 mins), G Gelderbloom for Smith (77 mins).

Munster: D Crotty; J O'Neill, R Henderson, J Holland, J Kelly; R O'Gara, P Stringer; P Clohessy, F Sheahan, J Hayes; M Galwey (capt), P O'Connell; A Quinlan, A Foley, D Wallace. **Replacements:** J Blaney for Sheahan (temp 18–30 mins), J Williams for Foley (53 mins), M Horan for Clohessy (62 mins), M O'Driscoll for O'Connell (62 mins), J Staunton for Crotty (68 mins), M Mullins for Henderson (68 mins).

Leicester scorers: Tries: Murphy, Healey; Conversion: Stimpson; Penalty: Stimpson

Munster scorer: Penalties: O'Gara (3).

2002–2003

Pool stage

12 October 2002 Gloucester 35 Munster 16

19 October 2002 Munster 30 Perpignan 21

6 December 2002 Munster 64 Viadana 0*

14 December 2002 Viadana 22 Munster 55

11 January 2003 Perpignan 23 Munster 8

18 January 2003 Munster 33 Gloucester 6

Quarter-final

13 April 2003 Leicester Tigers 7 Munster 20

Munster: J Staunton; J Kelly, M Mullins, R Henderson, A Horgan; R O'Gara, P Stringer; M Horan, F Sheahan, J Hayes; D O'Callaghan, P O'Connell; J Williams, A Foley, A Quinlan. **Replacements:** J Holland for Henderson (79 mins), M O'Driscoll for O'Connell (80 mins).

Munster scorers: Tries: O'Gara, Stringer; Conversions: O'Gara (2); Penalties: O'Gara (2)

Semi-final

26 April 2003 Toulouse 13 Munster 12

Munster: J Staunton; J Kelly, M Mullins, R Henderson, A Horgan; R O'Gara, P Stringer; M Horan, F Sheahan, J Hayes; D O'Callaghan, P O'Connell; J Williams, A Quinlan, A Foley. **Replacement:** J Holland for Henderson (80 mins).

Munster scorer: Penalties: O'Gara (2); Drop goals: O'Gara (2)

2003–2004

Pool stage

6 December 2003 Bourgoin 17 Munster 18
13 December 2003 Munster 51 Treviso 0
10 January 2004 Gloucester 22 Munster 11
17 January 2004 Munster 35 Gloucester 14
24 January 2004 Treviso 20 Munster 31
31 January 2004 Munster 26 Bourgoin 3

Quarter-final

10 April 2004 Munster 37 Stade Français 32
Munster: C Cullen; J Kelly, M Mullins, R Henderson,
S Payne; R O'Gara, P Stringer; M Horan, F Sheahan,
J Hayes; D O'Callaghan, P O'Connell; J Williams (capt),
A Foley, D Wallace. **Replacements:** A Horgan for Mullins
(65 mins), J Flannery for Williams (71–80 mins),
J Holland for Kelly (80 mins). **Sin-binned:** Sheahan
(71 mins).
Munster scorers: Tries: Payne, Henderson, Mullins,
Horan; Conversions: O'Gara (4); Penalties: O'Gara (3)

Semi-final

25 April 2004 Munster 32 Wasps 37
Munster: C Cullen; J Kelly, M Mullins, R Henderson,
S Payne; R O'Gara, P Stringer; M Horan, F Sheahan,
J Hayes; D O'Callaghan, P O'Connell; S Keogh, A Foley,
J Williams (capt). **Replacements:** J Holland for O'Gara
(29 mins), A Horgan for Keogh (78 mins). **Sin-binned:**
D O'Callaghan (63 mins), Henderson (72 mins).
Munster scorers: Tries: Foley, Williams; Conversions:
Holland (2); Penalties: O'Gara (3), Holland (3)

2004–2005

Pool stage

23 October 2004 Munster 15 Harlequins 9
31 October 2004 Neath-Swansea Ospreys 18 Munster 20
3 December 2004 Castres Olympique 19 Munster 12
11 December 2004 Munster 36 Castres Olympique 8
8 January 2005 Munster 20 Neath-Swansea Ospreys 10
15 January 2005 Harlequins 10 Munster 18

Quarter-final

3 April 2005 Biarritz Olympique 19 Munster 10
Munster: S Payne; J Kelly, M Mullins, R Henderson,
A Horgan; P Burke, P Stringer; M Horan, F Sheahan,
J Hayes; D O'Callaghan, P O'Connell; A Quinlan,
D Wallace, A Foley. **Replacements:** J Holland for Burke
(74 mins), J Williams for Quinlan (76 mins), P Devlin
for Mullins (80 mins).
Munster scorers: Try: Wallace; Conversion: Burke;
Penalty: Burke

2005–2006

Pool stage

21 October 2005 Sale Sharks 27 Munster 13
Munster: S Payne; J Kelly, B Murphy, G Connolly,
A Pitout; R O'Gara, T O'Leary; M Horan, F Sheahan,
J Hayes; D O'Callaghan, M O'Driscoll; A Quinlan,
D Leamy, A Foley (capt). **Replacements:** J Flannery
for Sheahan (43–48 mins and 73 mins) and for Hogan
(56–64 mins), T Hogan for Quinlan (49 mins),
F Pucciariello for Hayes, D Wallace for Leamy, P Stringer
for O'Leary (all 73 mins). **Not used:** J Manning,
R Henderson. **Sin-binned:** Sheahan (51 mins).
Munster scorers: Try: Sheahan; Conversion: O'Gara;
Penalties: O'Gara (2)

29 October 2005 Munster 42 Castres Olympique 16
Munster: S Payne; J Kelly, G Connolly, T Halstead,
A Horgan; R O'Gara, P Stringer; M Horan, J Flannery,
J Hayes; D O'Callaghan, M O'Driscoll; D Leamy,
D Wallace, A Foley (capt). **Replacements:** F Pucciariello
for Hayes (55 mins); B Murphy for Connolly (79 mins);
T Hogan for O'Driscoll, S Keogh for Foley, T O'Leary
for Stringer, J Manning for O'Gara, D Fogarty for
Flannery (all 80 mins). **Sin-binned:** Payne (75 mins).
Munster scorers: Tries: O'Callaghan, Flannery, Horgan,
Kelly, Halstead; Conversions: O'Gara (4); Penalties:
O'Gara (2), Manning

10 December 2005 Newport-Gwent Dragons 8
Munster 24
Munster: M Lawlor; J Kelly, G Connolly, T Halstead,
A Horgan; R O'Gara, P Stringer; M Horan, J Flannery,
J Hayes; D O'Callaghan, M O'Driscoll; D Leamy,
D Wallace, A Foley (capt). **Replacements:** B Murphy
for Connolly (77 mins), T O'Leary for Foley, F Roche
for Horan, D Fogarty for Flannery, T Hogan for
O'Callaghan, S Keogh for Leamy, J Manning for
O'Gara (all 80 mins). **Sin-binned:** Murphy (80 mins).
Munster scorers: Tries: Leamy, Horan; Conversion:
O'Gara; Penalties: O'Gara (2); Drop goals: Lawlor,
O'Gara

17 December 2005 Munster 30 Newport-Gwent
Dragons 18
Munster: S Payne; J Kelly, G Connolly, T Halstead,
A Horgan; R O'Gara, P Stringer; M Horan, J Flannery,
J Hayes; D O'Callaghan, M O'Driscoll; D Leamy,
D Wallace, A Foley (capt). **Replacements:** B Murphy
for Halstead (72 mins). **Not used:** D Fogarty,
F Pucciariello, T Hogan, S Keogh, T O'Leary,
J Manning. **Sin-binned:** Horan (75 mins).

Munster scorers: Tries: O'Driscoll, Foley, Flannery; Conversions: O'Gara (3), Penalties: O'Gara (3)

13 January 2006 Castres Olympique 9 Munster 46
Munster: S Payne; J Kelly, B Murphy, T Halstead, I Dowling; R O'Gara, P Stringer; M Horan, J Flannery, J Hayes; D O'Callaghan, P O'Connell; D Leamy, D Wallace, A Foley (capt). **Replacements:** T O'Leary for Kelly (53 mins), F Pucciariello for Horan, M O'Driscoll for O'Connell (both 61 mins), S Keogh for Foley (75 mins), J Manning for O'Gara (76 mins). **Not used:** G Connolly.
Munster scorers: Tries: Horan, Payne, O'Connell (2), O'Leary (2), Kelly; Conversions: O'Gara (3), Manning; Penalty: O'Gara

21 January 2006 Munster 31 Sale Sharks 9
Munster: S Payne; J Kelly, B Murphy, T Halstead, I Dowling; R O'Gara, P Stringer; M Horan, J Flannery, J Hayes; D O'Callaghan, P O'Connell; D Leamy, D Wallace, A Foley (capt). **Replacements:** M O'Driscoll for O'Connell, D Fogarty for Flannery, F Pucciariello for Horan, S Keogh for Foley, T O'Leary for Stringer, M Lawlor for Payne (all 80 mins). **Not used:** G Connolly.
Sin-binned: Horan (35 mins).
Munster scorers: Tries: Foley, Dowling, Murphy, Wallace; Conversions: O'Gara (4); Penalty: O'Gara

Quarter-final
1 April 2006 Munster 19 Perpignan 10
Munster: S Payne; J Kelly, T O'Leary, T Halstead, I Dowling; R O'Gara, P Stringer; M Horan, J Flannery, J Hayes; D O'Callaghan, P O'Connell; D Leamy, D Wallace, A Foley. **Replacements:** M O'Driscoll for Leamy (38 mins), J Manning for O'Gara, C Cullen for Dowling (both 80 mins). **Not used:** D Fogarty, F Pucciariello, S Keogh, R Henderson.
Munster scorers: Try: O'Connell; Conversion: O'Gara; Penalties: O'Gara (4)

Semi-final
23 April 2006 Leinster 6 Munster 30
Leinster: G Dempsey; S Horgan, B O'Driscoll, G D'Arcy, D Hickie; F Contepomi, G Easterby; R Corrigan, B Blaney, W Green; B Williams, M O'Kelly; C Jowitt, K Gleeson, J Heaslip. **Replacements:** E Miller for Jowitt (57 mins), R McCormack for Corrigan (69 mins).
Not used: D Blaney, N Ronan, B O'Riordan, K Lewis, R Kearney.
Munster: S Payne; A Horgan, J Kelly, T Halstead, I Dowling; R O'Gara, P Stringer; F Pucciariello,

J Flannery, J Hayes; D O'Callaghan, P O'Connell; D Leamy, D Wallace, A Foley (capt). **Replacements:** R Henderson for Kelly (14 mins), T O'Leary for Henderson (66 mins), F Roche for Foley (74 mins).
Not used: D Fogarty, M O'Driscoll, S Keogh, J Manning.
Sin-binned: Pucciariello (73 mins).
Leinster scorers: Penalties: Contepomi (2)
Munster scorers: Tries: Leamy, O'Gara, Halstead; Conversions: O'Gara (3); Penalties: O'Gara (3)

Final
20 May 2006 Munster 23 Biarritz Olympique 19
Munster: S Payne; A Horgan, J Kelly, T Halstead, I Dowling; R O'Gara, P Stringer; M Horan, J Flannery, J Hayes; D O'Callaghan, P O'Connell; D Leamy, D Wallace, A Foley (capt). **Replacements:** F Pucciariello for Horan (63 mins), M O'Driscoll for Foley (70 mins), A Quinlan for O'Connell (76 mins). **Not used:** D Fogarty, T O'Leary, J Manning, R Henderson.
Biarritz Olympique: N Brusque; J-B Gobelet, P Bidabe, D Traille, S Bobo; J Peyrelongue, D Yachvili; P Balan, B August, C Johnson; J Thion, D Couzinet; S Betsen, I Harinordoquy, T Lièvremont. **Replacements:** O Olibeau for Couzinet (45 mins), T Dusautoir for Lièvremont (52 mins), F Martin-Arramburu for Traille (53 mins), B Lecouls for Johnson (63 mins), B Noirot for August (67 mins), Johnson for Balan (72mins).
Not used: M Carizza, J Dupuy.
Munster scorers: Tries: Halstead, Stringer; Conversions: O'Gara (2); Penalties O'Gara (3)
Biarritz scorers: Try: Bobo; Conversion: Yachvili; Penalties: Yachvili (4)

PHOTO CREDITS